KU-273-610

A mouse in the soup...

Recipes and
stories from culinary
blogs

© 2007 Rebo International
This publication: © 2007 Rebo Productions b.v., Lisse

www.rebo-publishers.com
info@rebo-publishers.com

Contributors: Sylviane Beauregard, Dominique Bergès, Emmanuèle Carroué,
Véronique Chapacou, Claire Chapoutot, Mijo D'Araujo, Frédérique Despature,
Stéphanie Durand, Anne Lataillade,Gloria Herpin, Elvira Mendes André,
Jacqueline Mercorelli, Brigitte Munoz, Anne Rolland, Aude Toniello
Full-page photos: Raphaële Vidaling
Design: Claire Guigal
Original title: Une souris dans le potage… Recettes et récits de blogs culinaires
© 2006 Copyright SA, 12, Villa de Loucine, 75014, Paris, France
Translation: First Edition Ltd, Cambridge, UK
Editing: Sarah Dunham, Erin Slattery

ISBN: 978-90-366-2281-3

All rights reserved. Nothing in this publication may be reproduced and/or publicized
through the medium of print, photocopies, and microfilm, or by any other means, without
the prior written consent of the publisher.

A mouse in the soup...

Recipes and stories from culinary blogs

Contributors

Sylviane Beauregard, Dominique Bergès, Emmanuèle Carroué,
Véronique Chapacou, Claire Chapoutot, Mijo D'Araujo,
Frédérique Despature, Stéphanie Durand, Anne Lataillade,
Gloria Herpin, Elvira Mendes André, Jacqueline Mercorelli,
Brigitte Munoz, Anne Rolland, Aude Toniello

Full-page photos

Raphaële Vidaling

this way the blog acts as a shop window for the cook, allowing her talent and her creative abilities to be measured. In addition, it turns out to be a fantastic tool for organizing recipes, like a sort of interactive notebook with photos and comments built in.

There is now a real multilingual culinary blogosphere out there, with thousands of blogs. A closeknit virtual, or even very real, community for those who have become good friends! Their reasons for doing it? More than anything it is to share what they are doing with other enthusiasts, to get real feedback, and to get better at it… For sometimes a darling husband's comments are simply no longer enough for our bloggers, who are bursting with the desire to innovate and excel themselves!

Cookery blogs offer dishes that range considerably in terms of complexity. Some bloggers only upload "fancy" dishes, while others are at pains to show the failures as well as the triumphs. As a whole, they give us a glimpse of different styles of cooking, almost a kind of snapshot of "the woman in the kitchen." That is all this little book is trying to do: show you a sample of what is happening in the culinary blogosphere with fifteen different individuals, often with radically opposing ways of doing things. From Quebec to Guyana, our route takes you through world cuisine, cooking with spices or even organically, ending up with recipes that are more family focused—you are bound to recognize yourself in one of us!

Cafe Creole

Brigitte (Cayenne, French Guyana),
an inquisitive food lover

Exploring Guyana—adventures off the beaten track

Why this blog?

Born in the Périgord region of France, I have always
been at the geographical mercy of first my father's and
then my husband's job transfers. Having been forced
to travel all over the world, I became a real nomad at
heart. A chameleon then, I blend beautifully into the
country in which I live. I adapt to the customs and local
produce, enjoying meeting people and loving the colorful markets. I'm not afraid of speaking several different
languages, and if the words don't come, then it's down to the
hands…

> **My little weakness**
> Passion fruit!
> I start the day with a juice in the market; I often include it in desserts in the form of sor-bet, cream, tart, or fruit purees; and I flavor the local ti-punch drink with it…

A naturally curious chatterbox, I love swapping stories with as many people as I pos-
sibly can. The very nature of the blog was bound to suit me. The impetus for setting
up Cafe Creole was to stay in touch with my family and friends. We talk about recipes,
of course, but also about all those little everyday events like our walks and discoveries.
Gradually the readership began to grow in numbers and curiosity. Now I am often
asked questions by people who are in the process of coming to live here.

What kind of cuisine is it?

It is basically regional cooking using local produce available in the markets. I also take
advantage of the rich culinary traditions of this French département and the communities who live here: Brazilians, Surinamians, Haitians, Antilles folk, not forget-

ting the Asian influence of the H'mong community. Now that I feel more at home with the local produce, I am creating new recipes that are naturally inspired by existing ones.

A few examples of dishes

Wonderful wild shrimp, simply marinated and grilled, yam gratins and purees, fried plantain bananas, fish stews, wild boar fricassee, mango mousse, passion fruit sorbet, coconut biscuits, upside down figu banana cake for dessert…

What does that mean in an average day?

A trip to the fish market sets the tone. Then it's a matter of finding the vegetable or fruit that is going to make all the difference, not forgetting a visit to the woman who sells herbs and spices to get fresh cinnamon bark, kaffir lime leaves, or pretty (but fierce) chile peppers.

What's on the menu today?

A voyage of discovery around the colors and flavors Guyana has to offer. Get away on a flavorsome trip for your taste buds. So the menu will be made up of simple, fresh ingredients: avocado, shrimp, skate (which is plentiful around the Iles du Salut), and sweet pineapple that grows all year round…

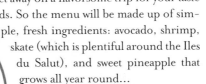

Advice from the blogger

If you want to be in turn a writer, photographer, and chef and if your computer is a faithful companion, then don't hesitate—enter the blogosphere!

Shrimp in coconut crumb dressing

When I was strolling on the beach, some coconuts with holes in them and the remains of some shrimp shells led me to imagine that little monkeys had been having a feast. What a good idea of theirs! Quite simply, this is how I came to create my shrimp in coconut dressing. A word of advice: they taste even better when eaten with your fingers while you plan a vacation.

Serves 4

- 2 lb (1 kg) large shrimp
- 4 limes
- 2 tbsp dry white wine
- 2 garlic cloves
- 2 eggs
- 1 bunch fresh coriander
- Flour
- 4 oz (100 g) packaged unsweetened coconut
- Oil for frying
- Salt and pepper

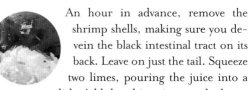

An hour in advance, remove the shrimp shells, making sure you devein the black intestinal tract on its back. Leave on just the tail. Squeeze two limes, pouring the juice into a dish. Add the white wine, crushed garlic cloves, salt and pepper. Mix it all well, and put the shrimp in the marinade. Cover the dish with plastic wrap and chill it for 1 hour in the refrigerator. Then heat the oil for frying, beat the eggs together, and chop the coriander. Put the flour in one small dish, the beaten eggs in another, and the coconut mixed with the chopped coriander in a third dish. Wipe the shrimp thoroughly. Dip them in the flour, then in the beaten eggs, and finally in the coconut and coriander mix. Press down well to make sure they are well covered in the dressing. Immerse the shrimp in a pan of hot oil and cook until they are golden brown, then drain them on absorbent paper. Serve hot, garnished with lime quarters and fresh coriander.

Cream of avocado soup with tomato sorbet

For the creamed soup (4 servings)
- 3 avocados, just ripe
- Juice of 1 lime
- 4 cups chicken stock
- 1 Caribbean chile pepper
- Chinese chives
- Salt and pepper

For the sorbet
- 2 cups tomato juice
- 2 tbsp confectioner's sugar
- 1/2 tsp five spice
- Basque chile pepper

For the pineapple
- 1/2 pineapple
- 1 knob of butter
- 2 tbsp confectioner's sugar

When the rainy season arrives in Guyana, the temperature drops by a few degrees, and the craving for some soup comes upon you. A slightly cooler evening is the ideal opportunity to serve this creamed soup. But, as the cold is all relative at our latitude (at worst, 80 °F / 27 °C), I've given the soup a sorbet garnish. One advantage at this time of year—the ice doesn't melt before it reaches the plates! At home in Guyana, the creamed soup is served warm on lovely summer evenings.

The day before, bring the tomato juice to a boil with the sugar and spices. Leave it to cool down, and then put it in the ice cream maker. Early the following day, cut the avocados in two and remove the flesh using a small spoon. Put it in the food mixer with the lime juice and the chicken stock. Whizz until smooth and creamy. Finely chop the chile pepper, taking care to remove all the seeds, and then add it to the soup. Season with salt and pepper and add the chopped chives. Mix together well and chill for at least 3 hours. Then peel the pineapple and cut it into little chunks. Melt the butter in a small frying pan and add the pineapple chunks. Cook for a few minutes, then sprinkle in the confectioner's sugar. Cook on high heat, stirring continuously to caramelize the pineapple without burning it. Leave it to cool down. Serve the creamed soup in a glass bowl with a scoop of sorbet, accompanied by pineapple croutons.

Cafe Creole
Lemongrass-scented skate

One day, by accident more than design, my husband caught a pretty large size skate. As the battle had been fought long and hard by both protagonists, our skate was giving off a rather strong smell. Having pleaded in vain for its life, asking for it to be put back in the water immediately, I had to resign myself to sharing my kitchen and my saucepans with it. Luckily, my ever obliging stalk of lemongrass whispered to me that it could be of assistance by flavoring the fish. It was over to me to do the rest, while my spouse was dispatched to the shower... lemon scented, of course.

Serves 4

- 2 stalks fresh lemongrass
- 4 skate wings
  (1 lb / 500 g flesh)
- 4 gelatin sheets
- 1 2/3 cups concentrated fish stock
- Fresh coriander
- Salt and pepper

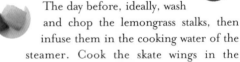

The day before, ideally, wash and chop the lemongrass stalks, then infuse them in the cooking water of the steamer. Cook the skate wings in the lemongrass steam, then leave them to cool down. Carefully remove the bones and keep the flesh. Soak the gelatin sheets in a little cold water. Heat the concentrated fish stock and add the well drained gelatin sheets. Stir well and adjust the seasoning. Pour a layer of gelatin into individual molds and put them in the freezer for 15 to 20 minutes. Then put a small amount of skate flesh on top and pour on another layer of gelatin. Put the molds back in the freezer. Continue this layering process. Just before the final layer of gelatin, place a few decorative leaves of coriander on top. Put in the refrigerator for at least 6 hours. Turn out the molds and serve with lime sorbet or, as in the photo, with small cubes of different colored bell peppers.

Madras curry ice cream with pineapple confit

I am a southern girl who has been bathed in Oriental spices since childhood. One day, however, curry came along, tantalizing my sense of smell and even making me betray my natural roots… To suggest curry in a dessert, I had to find a sweet companion for it, but one that was full of personality. Pineapple seemed equal to the task. Are you adventurous? Then follow me and you won't be disappointed.

For the ice cream (serves 4)

· 4 cups milk
· 3 tsp curry powder
· 8 egg yolks
· Generous 1 cup superfine sugar
· 5 oz (150 g) whipping cream
· A little lemon juice

For the confit

· 1 ripe pineapple
· 1/3 cup sugar
· 2 tbsp honey
· 1 piece fresh ginger about 3/4 in (2 cm) long
· 1 vanilla pod
· A pinch of Szechuan pepper

The day before, if possible, heat the milk and the curry powder. Leave it to infuse for 5 minutes. Beat the egg yolks and sugar until white and creamy, and then gradually stir in the warm milk. Put the pan back on the stove and thicken the mixture over gentle heat, stirring continuously. Remove from the heat as soon as it starts to boil. Leave to cool down at room temperature. Hand whip the cream and lemon juice together for 2 minutes. Fold them into the egg mix very gently. Pour the mixture into an ice cream maker or leave it in an ice cream tub in the freezer for several hours. The next day, peel and trim the pineapple, cut it into small pieces, and reserve the juice. Put the pineapple pieces, juice, sugar, honey, grated ginger, and vanilla pod (scraped out) into a copper bowl or a large saucepan suitable for slow cooking. Start cooking it on very low heat so that syrup forms gradually. Leave it to cook for about 1 hour. Halfway through cooking, add the pepper. Allow to cool down and serve as an accompaniment to the curry ice cream.

Chai Dumè

Yummy dishes from Dumè

Dominique (Bordeaux), a cook who draws her strength from her roots but gets inspiration from her wanderings

Why this blog?

A life of traveling, and a recent return to my roots, with a small winegrowing business that our family is rebuilding: such was the context for starting this blog. I wanted to talk about my life but also to find out more. So the topics covered will be linked together, for it's only a short step from the vineyard to the kitchen, isn't it? I've made some changes to suit cooks in all kinds of places. So, shall we begin? Come on then!

What kind of cuisine is it?

When you live in places where the tiniest oyster costs a fortune, or life is dictated by the arrival of the boat or plane, making all things relative, you quickly learn to make do—you experiment, you try things… and you end up finding some magical places where every culture and food sensation is represented, that is, in markets. In the stalls of Antilles women, the mixed race peasants of the West Indies and the stylized young women of Africa, in stalls well equipped for gastronomic challenges, you come across invaluable tips, and an assortment of individual ways of doing first rate local recipes. Having dreamed of asparagus in spring,

My little weakness

I love organizing big parties with a menu based on the wines of our vineyard. With red wine, dry white wine, and rosé from the estate, I am always able to create harmony in a menu that is well balanced.

mouna buns at Easter, chocolate at Christmas, fresh golden, crusty bread, Toulouse sausages with homemade mashed potatoes, foie gras… no matter when it was, I learned more often than not "on the job."

Dedication
Cooking is a labor of love. I dedicate this emotional cuisine to those who know the extent to which these colorful, fragrant dishes can combine refined delicacy and a lot of effort.

A few examples of dishes
A kind of culinary melting pot in which every ingredient, every recipe, and every smell is connected to a story, an individual or a smile: for me, cooking will always be Fidèle's vegetable pears, Wendy's rocket, Imalo's artistic sculpting of pineapple, the Horrible Little Man's bami, and—in retrospect—my grandfather's couscous or Mom's shorba soup.

What does that mean in an average day?
I savor moments in the kitchen: I have to make up for my daydreaming and reading by being ferociously organized, so all of these recipes can be prepared very quickly. The ritual of a harmonious table and the desire to share the fabulous moment with my guests gives me wings to fly!

What's on the menu today?
Simple recipes with tasty ingredients. I know there are not a lot of greens in there, but I'm working on it, honestly!

Carpaccio of duck breast with sesame breadsticks, roasted asparagus, and wasabi cream

It was in New Caledonia that I discovered marinated venison salad as well as the Japanese mustard called wasabi. Then, all I had to do was add some more, rather unusual but delicious, ingredients to this merry, cultural melting pot.

A little while in advance, put the duck breast into the freezer to firm it up. Remove the fat. Cut it into very thin slices. If necessary, cover the meat with plastic wrap and hit it firmly with a flat instrument. Arrange it on a dish. Mix 4 tablespoons of olive oil with a little chile pepper, the lemon juice, and the finely chopped shallots. Coat the carpaccio of duck with the dressing, sprinkle with chopped chives and Parmesan shavings, and leave it to marinate in the fridge for 20 minutes. To make the breadsticks, dissolve the dried yeast in 1 cup warm water and leave it for 10 minutes. Mix in the flour, oil, and salt. Knead the dough until it comes easily off the sides of the bowl. Leave it to double in size or for 1 hour in a warm place. Beat it down, flattening the dough well. Shape the breadsticks into the form of a pencil and roll them in sesame seeds. Put them on a baking sheet and allow them to double in size again for 1 hour in a warm place. Bake for 10 minutes at 480 °F (250 °C). Coat the asparagus in a little olive oil, then roast for 10 minutes at 200 °C (400 °F). Put the whipped cream on top mixed with the wasabi.

Carpaccios (4 portions)
- 1 duck breast
- 6 tbsp olive oil
- Basque chile pepper
- Juice of 1 lemon
- 2 gray shallots
- 1/2 bunch chives, chopped
- Parmesan shavings
- 2 lb (1 kg) green asparagus
- 1 cup whipping cream
- 2 tsp wasabi

For the breadsticks
- 1 tsp baker's yeast
- 1 lb (500 g) flour
- 3 tbsp olive oil
- 1/8 cup salt
- Toasted sesame seeds

Cream of chestnut soup with licorice and foie gras

This appetizer is one of our family favorites, but with so many variations that our guests may not necessarily recognize it, though they always enjoy it! Try, for example, replacing the licorice with a selection of dried morel mushrooms, or else serve the soup with little pastry shells filled with roast vegetables—an endive leaf or half a cabbage leaf caramelized with a little sugar— onto which fried slices of foie gras are laid.

For 4 servings

- 4 cups stock
- 1 lb (500 g) chestnuts, frozen or from a jar
- Generous 1/3 cup dry white wine
- 4 tbsp whipping cream
- Lemon juice
- 1 pinch powdered licorice
- 4 slices of fresh foie gras
- Salt and freshly ground pepper

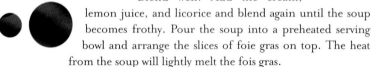

To the stock and add the chestnuts, white wine, salt, and pepper. Bring to a boil and simmer gently for about 15 minutes. Turn off the heat. Blend well. Add the cream, lemon juice, and licorice and blend again until the soup becomes frothy. Pour the soup into a preheated serving bowl and arrange the slices of foie gras on top. The heat from the soup will lightly melt the fois gras.

Flaked salt cod with navy beans

I put my skills in regional cuisine to good use for this dish, while adding my own two cents worth. In the end, the special magic of "cooking from the heart" had its effect and produced astonishing results. This new alliance became a marriage of love… according to my guests. As every marriage is individual and unique, don't hesitate to give this hearty dish your own personal touch with whatever is available in the market!

Serves 6

- I lb (500 g) white navy beans (tarbais if available)
- I lb (500 g) salt cod fillet
- I onion studded with cloves
- I piece of pork rind
- I carrot
- I bouquet garni and parsley stalks
- Peppercorns
- Ginger
- A few Toulouse sausages
- 2 onions
- Oil
- 3 or 4 beefsteak tomatoes
- A pinch of sugar
- Crushed olives
- Pine nut kernels
- Garlic, parsley, coriander
- Basque chile pepper

Soak the beans in advance for at least 12 hours. Desalt the cod by soaking it in cold water for a few hours, changing the water frequently. Rinse the beans and blanch them in boiling water for a few minutes. Drain and pour them into a stewpot, covering them with boiling water. Add the cloved onion, pork rind, carrots chopped into circles, the bouquet garni, and parsley stalks, a few peppercorns, and a little ginger. Do not add any salt as this will prevent the beans from cooking properly. Cook in the oven at 300 °F (150 °C) for about 2 hours, keeping it gently boiling, and add the sausages 30 minutes before the end. Poach the cod in simmering water for 10 minutes. Brown the onions in a little oil. Add the tomatoes (chopped into quarters), sugar, crushed olives, and dry toasted pine nut kernels. Spread the pork rind on the bottom of a dish, then the cod and bean mixture, the rest of the sauce, the sausages, a garlic clove, some parsley and coriander, chile pepper, and as much stock as you want. Cook in the oven for 30 minutes.

Childhood candy of lychee and raspberry

These smells from all corners of the world blend together for me into a happy memory of when I was a child. Going back to childhood by this route takes a bit of time, admittedly, but believe me, it's worth the effort!

Serves 8

- I 1/2 cups ground almonds
- 2 cups confectioner's sugar
- 6 whites and 4 yolks
- 6 sheets gelatin
- I vanilla pod
- 2 cups milk
- I tbsp cornstarch
- 5 drops rose essence
- I lb (500 g) lychees
- Generous I cup raspberry coulis
- Butter and flour for the baking sheet

At least 12 hours in advance, mix the ground almonds and I cup sugar. Beat the 6 egg whites until they form stiff peaks. Gently fold in the almond and sugar mixture. Make two circular shapes II in (28 cm) in diameter by pouring the mixture into cake rings on a buttered and floured baking sheet. Bake the rings for 7 minutes at about 350 °F (180 °C), checking often. Soften 3 sheets of gelatin in a bowl of cold water. Drain them well and melt them in hot coulis. Put the mixture in the fridge until it has set. Soften the remaining 3 sheets of gelatin in a bowl of cold water. Beat the 4 egg yolks with the remaining sugar until white and creamy. Heat the milk together with the scraped out vanilla pod and pour it onto the mixture, stirring all the time, and add the cornstarch. Keep stirring the cream continuously, while removing and squeezing out the gelatin sheets. Put them in the mixture and stir until they have dissolved. Do not allow the cream to boil. Add the drops of rose essence to the mix, mixing in well. Peel the lychees and cut them into halves. Put the first ring on the work surface. Spread the raspberry coulis on it and chill. Put the lychees on top. Spread on the creamy custard and cover it with the second ring. Leave it to set for several hours in the fridge, and then serve.

Clea Cuisine

Clea cuisine
For better and for worse...

Claire (Grenoble)
Japanese at heart

Why this blog?

I started my blog while I was still living in Japan and had but one wish—to penetrate the secrets of Japanese culture through its cooking! So I set about publishing recipe after recipe and discovered a very nice community of bloggers who were more than happy to welcome me and give advice on my failures and misguided ways in the kitchen... When I returned to France I also went back to my roots with my mother's organic vegetarian cooking, which from then on characterized most of my recipes.

What kind of cuisine is it?

Clea cuisine tends to be an organic blog, often vegetarian and what some would call health food. I would agree with them if you define health as the act of enjoying yourself while you eat... not to mention indulging your mind and body as well. Influenced by Japanese cooking, I prefer to use vegetable based products (soy milks, oats, rice...) as well as fermented foods like rice miso, soy sauce...), wholegrain cereals, and of course fruits and vegetables. A few "magical" products like agar-agar, a Japanese seaweed that substitutes for gelatin, or nutritional yeast that gives a cheesy taste to even the

> **My little weakness**
> Lemon in desserts! Lemon crumble, lemon tart, lemon bars, lemon and mango tart... Even talking about it makes my mouth water!

30

most lactose-free gratins, do not hold any secrets for me any more! The most important thing is not to get bored… and to cook like a real connoisseur of good food.

Advice from the blogger

I love making your mouth water—the photo is the key to a successful posting! You have to try out things with your camera in natural light, and don't be afraid to zoom in until the lens itself is beginning to drool!

A few examples of dishes

Squash and pine nut terrine, muffins with chestnut cream swirls, bread slices with melting carrots and marinated goat's cheese, little chocolate and ginger creams with agar-agar…

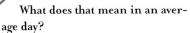

What does that mean in an average day?

I have become so organized that my boyfriend Ludo calls me Monica, like the star of the *Friends* series who organizes anything that moves! The list of courses is now my bible, and I am bursting with ideas that I jot down as I go along so that I don't forget them…

What's on the menu today?

With this menu, I am taking you on a long journey from the Savoy mountains, where I come from, to Japan, where we'll find out about the flavors of tofu and soy milk. We will then come back to the snow-covered mountains and heat ourselves up a bit…

Palm leaf cookies with green lentil caviar and goat's cheese

I love spreads, pates, caviars... But cold meats and fish eggs are off the menu here: mine are vegetarian dreams, with a melting cheese spread and lentil caviar with a surprising taste... Serve as a hors d'oeuvre with nut cups and cubes of Gruyere cheese.

Serves 4

· 1/2 cup green lentils
· 2 tbsp nutritional yeast
· 3 tbsp olive oil
· 1 tsp soy sauce
· 1 roll of puff pastry
· 1 goat's cheese log

Wash and cook the lentils for 25 minutes after bringing to a boil in three times their volume of water. Drain the lentils and mix in the yeast, oil, and soy sauce until you have a creamy paste. Roll out the puff pastry and cut out the biggest square you can from it. Spread the lentil caviar over the whole pastry shape. Cut the goat's cheese into thin circles and place them evenly on top of the caviar. Roll up the right side of the pastry into the middle of the square. Do the same with the left side, making two rolls that meet in the middle. Cover with plastic wrap and leave in the fridge for 30 minutes. Preheat the oven to 350 °F (180 °C). Take the roll from the fridge and cut into thin slices. Put them on a baking sheet, not too close together, as they will expand in size as they cook! Bake in the oven for 10–20 minutes until the cookies are puffed up and golden. You can eat them hot, warm, or cold, preferably the same day.

Winter squash salad and tofu kebabs

The Japanese are mad about winter squash, or kabocha as they call it—they are full of excellent ideas on how to use it, most notably in a salad with mayonnaise. I had the idea of a light version with a vegan mayonnaise whose subtle flavor of soy milk and mustard lends it a slightly more elegant touch.

For the salad
(4 portions)
· 14 oz (400 g) winter squash
· 3 tbsp soy milk
· 1 heaped tbsp whole grain mustard
· Olive oil
· Superfine sugar
· Salt and pepper

For 8 kebabs
· 10 oz (300 g) firm tofu
· 6 tbsp soy sauce
· 2 red bell peppers
· 4 tbsp mustard seeds
· 4 tbsp nutritional yeast
· 4 tbsp flour
· Olive oil

For the salad, cut the squash into large chunks and steam it for 30 minutes. Drain and peel it. Put 2 tablespoons of soy milk and the mustard into a large bowl. Gradually blend in the olive oil, a drop at a time, using an electric mixer until it has the consistency of mayonnaise. Season with salt and pepper. Chop the squash into bite-size chunks and add to the mayonnaise sauce. Add a pinch of sugar and the rest of the soy milk. Chill until ready to serve.

For the kebabs, cut the tofu into 40 cubes and put them onto a shallow plate. Pour over the soy sauce. Leave it to marinate for 20 minutes, turning the tofu so that it is well soaked. Peel the bell peppers and cut them into rectangular slices. Mix the mustard seeds, yeast, and flour on a plate. Roll the tofu in this mixture. Stick 5 tofu cubes and 4 pieces of pepper alternately on wooden skewers. Heat the olive oil in a large frying pan. Place the kebabs in it and cover. Cook for 15 minutes, turning regularly until golden brown all over. Serve hot with the salad.

Vegetable gratin with soy milk

This gratin is both light and full of different flavors: the natural taste of the vegetables is brought out by the accompanying delicacy of the milk and the soy cream. Vegetables have never tasted so good! There's a good case for forgetting about heavy bechamel and other buttery sauces once and for all! Why cover them up when you can reveal them?

Serves 4

- 2 potatoes
- 2 heads of broccoli
- 8 champignons de Paris
- I vegetable stock cube
- 4 tbsp flour
- I tsp curry powder
- Superfine sugar
- Generous ? cup soya cream
- 2/3 cup soy milk
- I egg yolk
- 4 oz Gruyere or Parmesan
- Olive oil
- Salt and pepper

Peel, wash, and dice the potatoes. Wash and divide the broccoli into small florets. Steam the potatoes and broccoli for 25 minutes. Trim the mushroom stalks, then peel and cut them into slices. Fry in olive oil until they are soft and no juice remains. Preheat the oven to 400 °F (200 °C). Crumble the stock cube into fine powder in a bowl. Add the flour, curry powder, salt, pepper, and a pinch of sugar. Mix well. In another bowl, mix the cream and soya milk. Gradually add these to the first bowl, stirring well. Finally add the egg yolk and the mushrooms. Put the well drained vegetables into a gratin dish, followed by the sauce, and then sprinkle with grated cheese. Bake in the oven for 20–30 minutes till the top of the gratin is a lovely golden brown.

Heartwarming chilled pears in hot snow

This little hot-and-cold dessert (or rather warm and frozen!) lets us round off the meal on a light note. By using agar-agar—Japanese seaweed—we can have a truly vegetarian dessert, not the case with gelatin. Adapt this dessert to the rhythms of the seasons by substituting apples for the pears in winter, or soft red fruits in summer.

Serves 4

2 pears
Generous 1/2 cup water
2 cups good quality pear juice
1 tsp ground cinnamon
1 tsp agar-agar
2 egg whites
1 tablespoon ground almonds
2 tbsp superfine sugar

Peel the pears, cut them into halves, and steam them for 10 minutes. Slice and arrange each half pear in a ramekin dish. Mix the water and pear juice in a pan, adding the cinnamon and agar-agar and stirring continuously. Bring to a boil and boil for 1 minute, then remove from the heat. Pour into the ramekins. Leave them to cool down for a few minutes, then put in the fridge for at least an hour. Before serving, whisk the egg whites into stiff peaks, adding the ground almonds and sugar just before the end. Divide the meringue mix into the ramekins. Set the oven to grill and brown the meringues till golden (2 or 3 minutes should be enough). Serve immediately.

épices et compagnie...

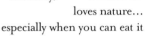

Spices & Company
The spice blog of an apprentice chef
in Germany Aude

(Cologne,
Germany)

loves nature…
especially when you can eat it

Why this blog?
When I came to Germany, I was looking for a fun task to brighten up my long days of searching for a job. At the end of 2004, I found out what a culinary blog was, quite by chance, and began reading the output of my future colleagues. A month later, I launched into it myself. To begin with, it was really just a novel way of keeping in touch with family and friends in France. I had no idea how it would all turn out eventually… The name "Spices & Company" gives a hint of what I expect from cooking: sharing, and going on a voyage of discovery. It was an ideal

My little weakness
There's nothing quite like candied chestnuts, a little pot of chestnut puree, or a dessert made with chestnut flour to break my resolve.

excuse to immerse myself in a world of spices every day, delving deeper into this vast, exciting subject. This is how sumac, long pepper, tonka bean, and company insinuated themselves into my life little by little.

What kind of cuisine is it?
My style of cooking is intuitive. I never know in advance what I am going to eat for the next meal. When I am hungry, I open my

cupboards, or fridge and have a look at my spice collection. My brain then goes into overdrive, sometimes coming up with nice things—more often than not desserts, or now and again an inspiring German dish.

Advice from the blogger

Don't have the latest digital camera and fully fitted kitchen? Great, you have satisfied the conditions for creating your culinary blog! Get ready now to make some new friends.

A few examples of dishes

Shrimp colombo in coconut milk, duck paddling in sauerkraut; mackerel and glasswort salad; apricot and amarettini cheesecake; milk spread with marzipan; pears poached in rose, lemongrass and vanilla; lavender wafer cookies...

What does that mean in an average day?

I spend most of my spare time in the smallest room in my apartment—my 30 sq ft (2.8m2) kitchen—or with my nose in cookbooks. When friends come to dinner, they help with the photo shoot of their plates. When I am someone else's guest, I always leave with one or two of the host's cookbooks. And at midday, I no longer take a lunch break, but have a blog break!

What's on the menu today?

In today's recipes, there is a whiff of Italy (a reference to my distant heritage), lots of vegetables (to grow big and strong!), a few inevitable spices, and a great dessert to finish—else it wouldn't be a proper meal!

Little canapé turnovers

Munch at random and find out what's inside. These little Italian-style turnovers are delicious warm. If you make them in advance, cook them for at least 2 or 3 minutes, then reheat them in the oven for a few minutes before serving the hors d'oeuvre.

For 20 turnovers

- 2 tsp baker's yeast
- 7/8 cup flour
- Olive oil
- Salt
- 2 tbsp pine nut kernels
- A small handful of basil leaves
- 2 oz (40 g) Serrano ham
- 1 oz (30 g) small artichoke hearts in oil
- 10 black olives, pitted
- 3 oz Provolone cheese

Dissolve the yeast in 2 teaspoons of water. If using active dry yeast, follow the maker's instructions. Put the flour in an earthenware dish. Form a well and pour in the dissolved yeast with 1 1/4 cups water. If using active dry yeast, follow the maker's instructions. Mix together and then add 1 tablespoon olive oil and 2 pinches of salt. Knead the dough and make it into a ball, then set it to one side. Preheat the oven to 350 °F (180 °C). Finely chop the pine nuts, basil, ham, artichoke hearts, and olives. Mix them all together. Grate the cheese and add the rest of the ingredients. Roll out the dough on a floured work surface until very thin. Cut out circles 2–3 in (6–7 cm) in diameter using a pastry cutter or a tumbler. Place a teaspoonful of filling into the middle of each circle and close them up in a semicircle or pyramid shape, pinching the edges together to seal it well. Put the turnovers on a baking sheet lined with wax paper. Brush with olive oil and bake in the oven for 25 minutes. Serve warm.

Cream of cauliflower and parsnip soup with crispy coppa sausage

This recipe is for all of us who are fed up with cauliflower cheese! In winter this creamed white vegetable soup is ideal for warming up your guests when the log fire refuses to catch or the radiators are not working. Its lightly seasoned flavor and the crispy coppa stimulate the appetite for what's still to come...

Serves 4

- 2 small garlic cloves
- Olive oil
- 3/4 lb (350 g) cauliflower
- 7 oz (200 g) parsnip
- Salt
- 3 slices coppa sausage
- 2 tbsp mascarpone
- Pinch of Basque chile pepper
- 3 tbsp grated Parmesan
- Basil leaves

Brown the crushed garlic in a tablespoon of olive oil in a casserole dish. Add the cauliflower broken into florets and the peeled parsnip, chopped into slices. Brown for 2 minutes on high heat, stirring continuously. Add 1/2 teaspoon salt and 1 2/3 cups water. Cover and let it simmer for 20 minutes. In the meantime, chop the coppa sausage slices into pieces and broil on a hot grill for 1 min. Blend the vegetables, add the mascarpone, chile pepper, and Parmesan, and mix well. Adjust the seasoning. Serve sprinkled with crispy coppa bits and basil leaves.

Panfried salmon
and vegetables with lemongrass

Lemongrass goes perfectly with salmon. And I can't resist cumin. The baby vegetables are cooked al dente. And the sauce is a nod and a wink to a Portugese blogger I almost met on two occasions...

Serves 4
- 1 lb (500 g) fresh salmon
- 2 stalks lemongrass
  (or 2 × 2 in / 6 cm pieces)
- 1 tsp cumin seeds
- Olive oil
- 4 oz (125 g) baby sweet corns
- 9 oz (250 g) snow peas
- 5 small red onions
- 2 medium size zucchini
- 1/4 stick of butter
- 1/3 cup fish stock
- 3 tbsp port
- Ground salt
- White pepper

Arrange the salmon in a dish and cover with the finely chopped lemongrass. Add a pinch of salt, cumin, and two tablespoons of olive oil. Leave to marinate in the fridge for 1 hr 30 minutes. Cook the corn (15 minutes) and the snow peas (5 minutes) separately in boiling salted water. Chop 4 of the onions and the zucchini into slices. Thinly slice the remaining onion and brown it in butter in a small saucepan until golden. Add the fish stock and the port, reducing it by two thirds by fast boiling. In a frying pan, brown the onions in a tablespoon of oil with a pinch of salt. Add the zucchini and cook until tender, then add the peas and sweet corn. Panfry the salmon with the spices for 3–4 minutes each side. Arrange the vegetables on the plates and then place on the salmon, adding some pepper. Pour the sauce into the pan and simmer for 1 minute. Coat the plates with sauce. Serve immediately.

Tangerine tartlets with crystallized ginger and white chocolate sauce

A very effective dessert, at least as far as my neighbors are concerned, though it takes a bit of time when you stick to using fresh fruit. But the taste is worth it!

For 4 tartlets

- I egg yolk
- I tbsp superfine sugar
- I unwaxed tangerine (zest)
- I/2 cup flour
- I/2 stick slightly salted butter
- 6 tangerines with firm skins or 3/4 lb (350 g) tangerines in syrup, prepeeled (weight when drained)

For the caramel

- 4 tbsp superfine sugar
- I/8 stick slightly salted butter
- 2 tsp crystallized ginger

For the sauce

- 2 oz (60 g) white chocolate
- I tbsp milk
- I tsp balsamic vinegar

Beat the egg yolk, sugar, and tangerine zest. Add the flour and then the butter, cut into pieces. Rub together into a crumble mix, and then pull it together into a ball of dough. Chill in the fridge. Peel the tangerines down to the flesh with a knife or drain the fruits in syrup. Preheat the oven to 350 °F (180 °C). Put the fruit segments at the bottom of the buttered tartlet molds.

For the caramel, lightly brown the sugar on high heat, add the butter and the chopped crystallized ginger. Mix together, shaking the pan. Divide the caramel between the molds.

Roll out the pastry thinly on a floured work surface. Cut out circles with a pastry cutter and cover the tangerines. Pierce with a fork and bake in the oven for 22 minutes. Melt the chopped chocolate in a bain-marie, keeping aside a few pieces for decoration. Add the milk and vinegar. Stir well and leave in the bain-marie on very gentle heat. When you remove the tartlets from the oven, leave some of the cooking juice in a bowl. Put a few spoonfuls of chocolate sauce into it to loosen it a little. Take each tartlet out of the mold on a plate over the sink, working quickly to prevent your fingers getting burned with the juice. Coat with sauce and sprinkle with shavings of white chocolate.

Frais !

Fresh!

Cooking with Fred:
Sweet, savory, fresh, and seasonal,
sprinkled with humor and soaked in love

Frédérique (Paris),
IT engineer
redeployed in the kitchen

Why this blog?

With all my talk of cooking at home, in the office and with friends, I was exhausting everyone with my tales of courses, experiments, and recipes. I had become obsessed with the subject and was unstoppable! Something had to be done, for what can be more miserable than not being able to share your passion for something? OK, I may be exaggerating just a little, but the fact is that creating

My little weakness
When I was a little girl, my mother would often find me with my head in the mixing bowl, busy licking the leftovers of the cake mix she had just put in the oven… Now that I am a big girl, I still do this, but I can say that it's quite normal and that you have to taste everything (absolutely everything). No kidding!

this blog has allowed me to express myself at leisure on my favorite subject, in a domain where guys and girls are all just as mad (nuts, even) about cooking as I am. What bliss!

What kind of cuisine is it?

French cooking, simple but elegant, for which I always prefer to use fresh produce and whatever is in season, hence the title of the blog.

A few examples of dishes

Things I like best are vegetables, snacks, and appetizers. So you'll find the recipe for chocolate madeleines alongside cream of cauliflower soup, guinea fowl with young cabbage alongside winter vegetable crisps.

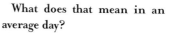

Advice from the blogger
Cooking is all about love, patience, and indulging in food. So to get some creative ideas, read all the blogs, devour the cooking magazines, and flick through all the books!

What does that mean in an average day?

Nothing terribly different: I have always been a real enthusiast for cooking and baking in fact, so the blog has not really increased my level of activity. On the contrary, now I have to take photos of all my accomplishments, which slows down the service a little when I have guests... Luckily they're very patient!

What's on the menu today?

The basic principle of all the recipes is to shake up old habits! You'll come across classics that escaped by one route, only to come back via other beaten tracks. It's fun, messing about with our usual way of doing things—it makes a nice change.

Minty petits pois supreme

Petits pois, mint... sounds familiar? Well, put your preconceptions aside as it's a fabulous combination. Serve these sweet little treats in vodka glasses as a hors-d'oeuvre or as a first course. It's subtle, original, and not too heavy, thanks to the miniformat—a kind of concentrated pleasure, really!

For the petits pois supreme (8 to 10 vodka glasses)

· I 1/3 cups shelled petit pois
· 1/2 cup white stock (veal or poultry)
· 6 tbsp whipping cream
· Lemon juice
· I whole egg + 2 egg yolks
· Salt and pepper

For the mint cream

· I shallot
· 1/8 stick butter
· 10 tbsp whipping cream
· Lemon juice
· 20 fresh mint leaves

Cook the petits pois in plenty of boiling salted water. Drain and blend with the veal stock, cream, a little lemon juice, the whole egg, and the egg yolks. Season with salt and pepper. Pass through a strainer to make a smooth cream. Preheat the oven to 180 °F (80 °C). Three quarter fill the vodka glasses with the mixture. Bake in a bain-marie for 30 minutes. Check that the mixture has set (to the consistency of egg custard), and if not, leave it a few more minutes. In the meantime finely chop the shallot. Brown lightly in the butter and add the cream and a little lemon juice. Reduce until it has thickened. Add the mint leaves, and then blend. For a very smooth texture, you can pass the mixture through a sieve. Pour the cream over the supreme. Serve warm with a long, slender spoon.

NB: my mother's trick for getting the right amount of cream on top of the glasses—use a pipette if you have one...

Salmon tartare with star anise and Parmesan crisps

We all know the absolute classic salmon tartare, but forget all the traditional versions and breathe new life into your recipe. In this one, the new idea is to use star anise. It is certainly reminiscent of dill, which is generally associated with salmon, but it has a more pronounced aniseed flavor! The final combination with Parmesan may surprise some of you, but the crunchiness of the crisps goes perfectly with the rich smoothness of the oily fish. On no account add any salt, however, as smoked salmon and Parmesan already take care of this, and besides, you'll have a perfect dish without any unsightly little white spots.

Serves 4
· 3/4 lb (350 g) fresh salmon
· 4 slices smoked salmon
· 2 star anise pods
· Basque chile pepper
· Freshly ground pepper
· Parmesan

Cut the smoked and fresh salmon into tiny cubes and mix well. Blend or grind the star anise pods, adding a little Basque chile pepper and ground pepper. Season the salmon with about half the spice mix. Mix together well; cover tightly so that the plastic wrap adheres to the salmon tartare, and leave to chill for at least 2 hours. You do not need to add salt. If you want a saltier flavor, add some extra smoked salmon. Arrange the grated Parmesan in little heaps on a silicon baking sheet or a nonstick tray. Press them

into circles with the back of a spoon and sprinkle them with the rest of the spice mix. Put under the grill in the oven until the Parmesan melts, but do not let it brown. Leave to cool on a rack. Serve the tartare with the chips.

Fresh!
Fake Provencal daube with cod

Daube (a rich casserole) is usually made with beef, so you may be surprised to find that this combination of white fish and red wine works wonderfully. Feel free to prepare the sauce in advance, as this will give you more time to organize the meal. Cooking the fish takes no time at all. All the advantages of a daube without the drawbacks really!

Serves 4

- 4 shallots
- Olive oil
- 6 sprigs of thyme
- 2 bay leaves
- 4 garlic cloves
- 2 cloves
- 3 cups red wine (Bordeaux)
- 1/2 unwaxed orange
- 2 1/3 cups veal (or poultry) stock
- 4 cod fillets
- A few black olives
- Freshly ground salt and pepper

Gently brown the shallots in a tablespoon of olive oil. Add the thyme, bay leaf, roughly chopped garlic, cloves, and red wine. As soon as it comes to a boil, burn it off to remove the acidity. Remove the peel from the orange, but be careful not to take off any of the pith (white part). Add to the sauce and reduce it by half. Add the veal stock and once again reduce by half. Strain and reduce the mixture on very low heat until it has a syrupy consistency. Put each cod fillet on a piece of parchment paper. Season with salt and pepper, and drizzle with olive oil. Close the parchment paper tightly. Steam or microwave the cod. When ready to serve, pour 2 tablespoons of olive oil over the wine sauce, whisking to ensure the mixture is well blended. Serve the cod fillet and sauce on the side along with a few black olives on a very hot plate.

Milk chocolate and praline gateau with praline custard

Or how to add a European touch to the excellent American brownie! The use of milk chocolate, given a lift by the nutty flavor of the praline, will come as a treat for sweet lovers, chocoholics (in spite of the absence of dark chocolate), and everyone else as well!

For the gateau
· Generous 1/2 stick butter
· 2/3 cup superfine sugar
· 4 oz (115 g) milk chocolate
· 2 eggs
· 2 oz (50 g) praline (paste or powder)
· Generous 1/2 cup flour
· 1 pinch salt
· 1 tsp baking powder

For the custard
· Generous 1 cup milk
· 1/2 cup whipping cream
· 3 egg yolks
· 5 tbsp superfine sugar
· 2 oz (50 g) praline (paste or powder)

Preheat the oven to 350 °F (175 °C). Soften the butter. Melt the chocolate in a bain-marie or in the microwave. Mix together the butter, sugar, and eggs. Add the melted chocolate and the praline. Sift together the flour, salt, and baking powder, then add to the mixture. Pour into a square mold. Bake for 35 to 40 minutes (depending on whether you prefer it soft or a little firmer). Make up the custard: bring the milk and cream to a boil. Mix the egg yolks and sugar but don't blanch them. Add the praline. Pour the boiling milk into the egg mixture, then put it all back in the pan. Cook, stirring continuously with a spatula until the custard has thickened (to the stage where a distinct trail will be left if you run your finger over the coated spatula; if you have a thermometer, this corresponds to 185 °F / 85 °C, no higher). Strain and cover with plastic wrap (laying the wrap directly on top of the custard). Chill and serve with the gateau, either warm or chilled.

Je mijote *Histoires gourmandes et parfois épicées de Mijo.*

Mijo (from the Poitou swamp),
smiling and curious,
as I simmer slowly

Simmering slowly...
Life consists of cold meats!

Why this blog?

In June 2004 I discovered the world of blogs: lots of personal entries, entries with photos, poetry, observations, as well as expat blogs. Being neither an expat nor an extrovert prepared to expose herself on a daily basis, I could not envisage myself as part of this world, until that fantastic day in September 2004 when I discovered two cooking blogs! I immediately took to this interactive idea—I give you my recipe and in return I expect your comments, observations, criticisms, and suggestions. It was not long until my blog was born.

What kind of cuisine is it?

Cooking that is simple, tasty, hearty, adventurous, and for all the family. Cooking to be enjoyed and that you enjoy doing. Good country cooking straight from the garden. It takes several pairs of hands, whether it's my children's or my husband's. For a long time I regarded pots and pans as simply a way of filling my stomach. Of course we had to eat, but I never liked following a recipe. My eldest son was born in January 1998. He would only eat a little tub

> **My little weakness**
> Cold meats from the deli! But I avoid eating them, preferring instead to talk about them and live on my memories.

Advice from the blogger

So you want to create your own blog? Keep the recipe instructions as simple as possible, describing every stage in detail.

of carrots, refusing all other prepre-pared dishes from the baby food shelf. A revelation. I suddenly became passionate about cooking, so that I could give him the best possible food. Since then we've all benefited from it, which I love! I like to browse, looking for new ideas so that we never eat the same thing twice. I like to listen to music while I'm cooking. I love to see my two sons tying on their aprons to help me, and then see all the contented faces after a good meal.

A few examples of dishes
Bruschetta with mozzarella, melon salad with feta cheese and toasted pine nuts, veal kebabs in Pineau wine with pink and green peppercorns, malfadine pasta with sage, redcurrants and mackerel...

What does that mean in an average day?
Greater pleasure from the desire to share, more carefully presented dishes for the photo break, children and a spouse who come up with ideas for dishes, hopping about together waiting for comments to find out if people liked it.

What's on the menu today?
An invitation to join us for an elegant but friendly evening meal, which the whole family has helped to prepare. For instance, your children will love getting the little sweets ready.

Creamed soup with caramelized onions

Soup is good. In our family, no one turns their nose up at a good bowl or plate of soup. That's why I love to try out different combinations of textures, colors, vegetables, and stocks. Guessing the ingredients has even become something of a game—for this soup, my husband joined in. He had trouble working out the hint of subtle fragrance that combined astonishingly well with the smoothness of the creamy stock and the caramelized onions. But he was both surprised and delighted at the successful combination with dry white vermouth.

Serves 4
- 4 large onions
- Butter
- 1 leek
- 3 garlic cloves
- 1/3 cup dry white vermouth
- 3 cups chicken stock
- Generous 1 cup whipping cream
- Salt and pepper

Peel and thinly slice 2 of the onions. Brown them very gently in a frying pan with a knob of butter for 45 minutes. They should become slightly caramelized. Stir occasionally, and when they are ready, cover them and put them to one side. Peel and thinly slice the remaining onions. Clean the leek, then cut the white and pale green parts into circles. Chop the garlic. In a large pan, brown the onions, leek, and garlic in a knob of butter, stirring continuously for 5 minutes. Lower the heat and continue to cook gently for about 10 minutes, stirring occasionally. Add the vermouth, chicken stock, salt, and pepper. Continue to cook gently for about 15 minutes. Remove from the heat and blend with a mixer, then add the cream. Put the pan back on the stove and bring almost to boiling point. Pour into bowls or soup plates and serve with a generous spoonful of caramelized onions in the center.

Duck breast with nuts

I will always remember Christmas Eve dinner in 1994. My first real sweet and sour dish and my first encounter with maple syrup! Without knowing it, my future mother-in-law had rocked my taste buds with her duck in maple syrup. This is certainly not the same recipe as the one of that Christmas Eve. My mother-in-law can't remember it and I've never dared to reproduce it for fear of not finding that magical moment of fla-vor once again. So I have tried to create an original recipe for duck breasts with crunchy nuts and a hint of maple syrup.

Serves 4
· 2 duck breasts
· Generous 1 cup shelled walnuts
· Generous 1 cup whole hazelnuts
· 5 tbsp maple syrup
· Salt and pepper

Preheat the oven to 400 °F (200 °C). Make lattice shape cuts across the skin of the duck. Season with salt and pepper. Heat a large fry-ing pan without adding any oil, then put the duck breasts in it, skin side down. Cook like this for 6 minutes. Turn the breasts over and continue to cook for 3 minutes on moderate heat. Put the breasts into an ovenproof dish. Crush the wal-nuts and hazelnuts and add the maple syrup. Spread this mixture over the duck breasts. Bake in the oven until the nuts are golden. Take the dish out of the oven and cover with aluminum foil. Leave it to rest for 5 minutes, then cut the breasts into slices. Serve with a simple potato mash.

A word of advice
Make a little more than you need so you'll have some leftovers for the next day. It's wonderful served cold. The duck breast and nuts will have had time to soak up the maple syrup.

Bittersweet chocolate souffle with orange blossom

While I have never made a cheese souffle, I enjoy making a souffle for dessert. It's staggeringly simple. It's good, and it's light and airy. You can prepare the custard mix in advance and put the oven on at the last minute. Then the final trump card: last minute guests will have arrived; everyone will be seated, and poised ready to grab their little spoons. The applause will come later. The souffle will sink back very quickly, but that's quite normal!

Serves 4

- Generous 1/2 cup milk
- 4 eggs
- 1/2 cup superfine sugar
- 1/2 cup flour
- 1/2 cup cocoa powder
- 1 tsp orange blossom water
- Butter for greasing

To make the custard sauce, heat the milk in a pan. Separate the whites of the eggs from the yolks and put the whites to one side. Whisk the sugar and egg yolks in a bowl till they are creamy white. Next add the flour, then the cocoa powder. Very gradually pour the boiling milk over the mixture, stirring well to stop the eggs from congealing. Pour it all into a pan and thicken it over low heat, stirring with a wooden spoon until it comes to a boil. Take it off the heat, then add the orange blossom water and allow the custard to cool down a little. Preheat the oven to 400 °F (200 °C). Whip the egg whites till they form stiff peaks. Carefully fold the whipped egg whites into the custard mix with a spatula. Grease the ramekin dishes with butter and fill them with the mixture. Bake in the oven for about 15 minutes, keeping a close eye on it. Serve immediately.

Blackberry bites

Now and then my children love to put their aprons on and help me to prepare the meal. These bites are very easy for little hands to make and guarantee thunderous applause! They will be so proud to offer you these sweet little morsels with such a delicate color—you can eat them as finger food when it's tea or coffee time.

Serves 4
· Generous 1/2 stick butter
· 20 sponge fingers
· 2 teaspoons blackberry syrup
  (homemade or bought)
· Superfine sugar

Melt the butter in a pan over gentle heat. Grate the sponge fingers into a mixing bowl. Pour the melted butter and the blackberry syrup onto the grated sponge fingers and mix together with a fork until it turns into a paste. Leave it to set for 30 minutes in the fridge. Scoop out small amounts of the paste with a teaspoon and make them into little balls with your hands. Then roll them in the sugar.

Bonus point: Olivier's homemade blackberry syrup
Crush the blackberries and leave them for 2–3 days in the fridge. Squeeze them through a muslin cloth, leaving the extracted juice overnight. The next day, skim the top of the juice. Measure the juice, adding 2 1/2 cups sugar for every 2 cups of juice. Pour it into a pan and bring it gently to a boil. Cook for 10 minutes. Skim the syrup, and then leave it to cool. Bottle it, cover with a piece of cloth and tie it up. Leave it in a cool place for 6 weeks, and then cork it properly. Store it in the fridge.

la cuiller en bois
la cuisine est un partage

The wooden spoon
Welcome to our table

Gloria (Libourne),
hectic grandmother,
addicted to coffee

Why this blog?

I started telling my colleagues about my cooking, with the help of photos. Lunching at our desks, we bring in things we have made, taste them, and swap recipes. For me, the blog was a natural extension of this, something that might be of interest to my family and friends. I'm still astonished at the extent to which it has taken off. I am very moved by all the exchanges and encounters that have followed as a result.

My little weakness
Coffee—my faithful companion throughout the day.

What kind of cuisine is it?

You could describe it as family fare, which for me conjures up the great feasts of my childhood—the kind of hearty regional cooking that I am far from mastering. I would call it "simple and everyday" cooking, as every cook can do it, even the most inexperienced. I am by no means an expert at specialized culinary techniques. I work with

basic food within the budget of an average household, throwing in a little curiosity about unusual products (not specially rare or expensive) and the use of spices. I adapt classical recipes so that I can surprise my guests without shaking the foundations of their culinary practices. The presentation and color play do the rest, giving a festive feel to any dish.

Advice from the blogger

Be yourself. Don't attempt a style of cooking that isn't you—and it won't stop you from trying out new flavors and experimenting.

A few examples of dishes

Apple cake, mutton stew with fresh figs, lasagna from freezer leftovers, zucchini stuffed with chicken and ricotta, sweet apple and fig bake, new wine jelly…

What does that mean in an average day?

After the hectic snapping in the first few months, my camera (always within reach) managed to blend unobtrusively into the background on the table. What I cook every day is not about being obsessed with the blog, making a dish every day just to put it on the web. On the contrary, my view of regional produce, the way we do things, and all our experiments has changed and I wonder if anyone would really be interested in it. This is the deciding factor in choosing articles. Now I am setting out to prove that cooking can be inventive, user friendly, and available to everyone.

What's on the menu today?

I'm always cooking in a rush, so I improvise and come up with different ideas all the time. For this menu, I have stuck to my usual habits. I wasn't inspired, maybe because of the pressure of a blank page in front of me. Ideas popped up too late and unexpectedly, in a spirit of impulsiveness and dissatisfaction. In retrospect now that the dust has settled, I can see that's what I am like, and I couldn't express myself any better.

Mini cheesecakes
with goat's cheese and cumin

What if I told you a secret? Two years ago I didn't know what cheesecakes were, not even the name. Surfing culinary sites on the web filled in the gaps in my knowledge and satisfied my curiosity, especially after getting to know Claire (Clea cuisine). Well known for her love of cakes, she encouraged me to try them out—sweet ones, of course, with or without pastry, plain, or with lemon. The idea of making a savory version soon began to preoccupy me. One day when I had nothing better to do, I awakened these desires by sprinkling a piece of goat's cheese with a pinch of cumin. So I threw myself into it, choosing a mini version more likely to seduce my guests. And here it is!

Serves 4

· 4 oz (100 g) cream cheese
· 4 oz (100 g) whipping cream
· Lemon juice
· 2 eggs
· 4 tsp cornstarch
· 3 oz (80 g) goat's cheese
· 1 tsp ground cumin

Preheat the oven to 325 °F (150 °C). Beat together the cream cheese, whipping cream, a little lemon juice, and the egg yolks. Mix the cornstarch in 3 tablespoons of water, and then add it to the mixture. Add the chopped goat's cheese and the cumin. Whisk the egg whites until stiff and fold them into the mixture. Pour into small molds. Bake for 15–20 minutes. Serve cold.

Tangy fruit in a glass

Have you ever woken up in the middle of the night with a flash of the obvious for an idea or recipe? That is what happened with this appetizer. At a time when I was lacking both inspiration and inclination, a bright idea came to me—mandarin segments and avocado in a glass! An explosion of colors... All I had to do was set off the explosion of flavors.

Serves 4
- 3 avocadoes
- 2 limes
- 8 mandarins
- 1 piece of ginger
- 12 large cooked shrimp

Dice the avocadoes. Grate the lime peel and squeeze the juice. Pour the zest and juice over the avocadoes. Put to one side. Peel 6 mandarins down to the flesh. Grate half of the piece of ginger and mix into the mandarins. Put to one side. Shell and slice the shrimp. Squeeze the juice of the second lime. Grate the rest of the ginger. Add these to the shrimp. Put to one side. An hour before serving, put the avocado, shrimp, and mandarins into the decorative glasses with their marinades. Squeeze the juice of the two remaining mandarins and divide it between the glasses. Chill until you are ready to serve.

Perch fillets with citrus vegetables

Loyal readers of my blog, I can hear you saying, "And what about Jean-Pierre?" As you can imagine, he has not been sitting idle, leaving me to do the cooking on my own! He has insisted on giving you one of his own creations, which is an excellent example of his approach to cooking—marinade, fish, steamed vegetables, cream, and white wine are the staples as far as he is concerned. That, along with the aim of keeping things simple and not spending too much time in the kitchen. You are also right in thinking that I would not pass on his recipe to you without adding my own 2 cents worth! If you like a recipe that is less "robust," you can leave out the potatoes.

Serves 4

- 4 perch fillets
- 2 large carrots
- 1 green bell pepper
- 1 red bell pepper
- 1 leek
- 1 lime
- 1 piece of ginger
- 4 large potatoes
- 2 tsps whipping cream
- A little lemon juice
- 2/3 cup white wine
- Chives
- Salt and pepper

Lay the fillets in a shallow dish. Add salt and pepper. Cover with the finely diced vegetables (carrots, bell peppers, and green part of the leeks). Prepare a marinade with the lime juice, a quarter of its finely chopped peel, and the grated ginger. Pour into the dish and leave to marinade overnight. Steam the vegetables from the marinade for 30 minutes. Boil the potatoes in salted water. Prepare a leek sauce with the white part of the leek, the cream, a little lemon juice, and the white wine. Fry the fish fillets in a pan. Arrange the fillets on the serving dish, add the sliced potatoes, and cover them with the leek sauce and the vegetables, dotted with chopped chives.

Tiramisu with prunes and lime curd

I've loved prunes ever since I was a child. It was my maternal grandmother who gave me a taste for them (along with a few other things…). As she has not been with us for a few years now, I was determined to end my meal with something from her. The idea of combining prunes and lemon had been simmering away in me for quite some time. You will definitely have some pureed prunes and lime curd left over, but I have not made a mistake about the amounts, I assure you. No, it's just to prolong the pleasure, for both of them will keep very well in the fridge!

Serves 4

· 1 lb (500 g) pitted prunes
· 2 cups black tea
· 1 1/2 cups superfine sugar
· 5 limes
· 1 tbsp cornstarch
· 6 eggs
· 5 oz (150 g) mascarpone
· 1–2 tbsp sugar cane syrup
· 12 small crepes

The day before, soak the prunes in the tea for about an hour. Drain them, reserving the tea, and cut them in half. Cook them on gentle heat, adding 2 tablespoons of sugar. Turn them into a puree by regularly adding the tea liquid, 3 tablespoons as a time, until the liquid has completely reduced. Add sugar to taste. Leave it to cool down. Also the day before, squeeze the juice of 4 limes and finely grate the rind. Heat gently with 2/3 cup sugar and the cornstarch. Add 4 beaten eggs, and cook until the mixture thickens, stirring continuously. Leave it to cool. Several hours in advance on the day of the meal, cream the yolks of the 2 remaining eggs with 1/2 cup sugar. Add the mascarpone and mix well. Beat the egg whites until stiff, and fold them into the mixture. Squeeze the juice of the last lime, adding the same amount of sugar cane syrup. Line the bottom of the glasses with the crepes. Pour in the syrup, soaking them. Arrange alternate layers of lime curd, puree, and cream. Chill for several hours. Serve with the remaining crepes.

La cuisine de Mercotte
Essais, réalisations et recettes au quotidien!

Mercotte's kitchen

Indulgent food is even better when it's shared

Mercotte
(Chambéry),
Confessed chocoholic

Why this blog?

Mainly to share a passion I have. A few days before setting up a blog, I was unaware of the existence of culinary blogs. I already had a few photos of my dishes on my personal web pages, but I could not integrate the recipes so it was a little frustrating. A reader told me about blogs, and I browsed a few in this book that were online at that time. *I was immediately captivated by the friendliness of swapping blog posts and comments, and so I threw myself into the process. As for the pseudonym Mercotte, it is the female version of Merc. This goes back to the time when my husband and I were a fearsome duo in car rallies. You've got it—Mercotte didn't always wear an apron. In the 1970s, it was more often a crash helmet in the middle of the Moroccan desert!*

> **Advice from the blogger**
> Just a single word—organization. Stay calm, plan well in advance, and everything will fall into place. No more last minute panics!

What kind of cuisine is it?

Mercotte's kitchen is a blog that focuses on desserts and chocolate in particular. Being able to reproduce chefs' recipes, matching up flavors and colors, and creating new recipes from classical bases are all a constant challenge. So to compensate, I also try to offer light appetizers. Some fish recipes, a few meat dishes, but I'm watching my health! My aim is also to demystify recipes for festive occasions that some people find too intimidating, by explaining them step by step and as clearly as possible.

A few examples of dishes
White chicken meat stuffed with prunes or foie gras, scallops layered with salmon, tuna tartare Thai-style, monkfish fricassee with baby vegetables, crunchy chocolate heaven, mascarpone mousse with seasonal fruits, almond cookie party…

What does that mean in an average day?
Life at breakneck speed concentrating on this passion of mine, the constant quest for creativity, a camera always within reach, organizing foodie weekends with cooking lessons (I've converted guest rooms in my house for this), an alarm call at 4 a.m. to prepare tasty little breakfasts for my students… and fridges in every room, under the stairs, and even in every bedroom!

What's on the menu today?
A menu favoring flavors—truffle, tamarind, kafir lime, and cardamom, and of course the inevitable chocolate, turned into a tangy candy.

My little weakness
Chocolate applied in every way, from savory to sweet. I aim for perfection so that I can share my passion better with everyone.

Warm scallop salad with leek mousse and truffle vinaigrette

Mmm, truffles! I would sell my soul for them. My trick of the trade? I buy them fresh when they are fully ripe, just when the moon changes between the end of January and the beginning of February. I clean them under running water with a soft brush to get rid of any traces of soil, and then leave them to dry for a few hours on paper towels. I then wrap them individually in aluminum foil before freezing them.

Serves 4

· 2 tbsp lemon juice
· 2 tbsp truffle juice
· 4 tbsp olive oil
· I small truffle (optional)
· I shallot
· 2 large leeks (white parts only)
· 1/2 stick butter
· 2 tbsp thick cream
· Sprigs of chervil for decoration
· 12 scallops
· Cayenne pepper
· Salt and pepper

Prepare the truffle vinaigrette a few hours in advance: mix the lemon juice, truffle juice, olive oil, finely diced truffle (if using), and salt and pepper in a small pan. Leave until it reaches room temperature. Finely slice the shallot and leeks. Sweat the shallot in butter in a saute pan but do not let it brown. Then add the leeks, season, cover the pan, and cook on low heat for about IO minutes. Blend well with the cream, adjusting the seasoning if required. Arrange the leek mousse on hot plates using ring molds and garnish with chervil. Warm up the vinaigrette. Season the scallops with salt, pepper, and cayenne, and then fry them quickly in olive oil in a very hot, nonstick pan for I minute on each side. Arrange them next to the mousse, pour on a little vinaigrette, and eat immediately.

Red mullet fillets with tamarind sauce and Oriental-style black rice

These days black rice is my fetish food for the cooking workshops I run in my house. If I tell you that it used to be known as "forbidden rice" in China, does that tempt you? Actually the emperors kept it for themselves for its nutritional value and its aphrodisiac properties. Today it is grown in the Po Valley in Italy. Food for your conversations, as well as your guests...

For 4 servings of fish
- Generous 1/3 cup light cream, 15% fat
- 1 tbsp tamarind paste
- 1 tbsp black olive tapenade (homemade if possible)
- 8 red mullet fillets

For the rice
- 1/2 cup black rice
- 1 carrot
- 1 cup fresh green beans
- Olive oil
- 1 cup frozen peas
- 1 small garlic clove
- A small amount of kafir lime zest
- A pinch of freshly grated ginger
- Salt

Cook the rice in a rice cooker or using the traditional method for 18 minutes, then drain and let it cool. Chop the carrot and beans into small pieces. Boil the vegetables separately in salted water until cooked but still crunchy, then run them under cold water and drain them. Just before the meal, fry the rice in olive oil with the vegetables, the crushed garlic, kafir lime, and ginger. Season with salt and pepper. Pile the rice into the ramekin dishes. Heat in the microwave if required and turn onto the plates to serve. Bring the cream to a boil and reduce it for 5 minutes. Mix in the tamarind and tapenade, whisking it all the time. In the meantime quickly fry the fish fillets (seasoned and descaled) skin side first. Coat the hot plates with sauce, and then lay the fillets on top in fan formation with skin side up.

Fresh fruit sundaes

If you are like me, you won't be able to see past dark chocolate and will even claim that white chocolate isn't chocolate at all. But, keep your preconceived notions to yourself long enough to taste the white version transformed into a tangy mousse—then tell me what you think! I've given both winter and summer variations, depending on which fruits are in season. But remember that it must be made the night before!

Serves 4

- Juice of 4 limes + zest of one lime
- 1/2 lemon (juice only)
- 4 tbsp mineral water
- Generous 2 tbsp superfine sugar
- 2 sheets gelatin
- 9 oz (250 g) raspberries (summer) or 2 pink grapefruits (winter)
- For the mousse
- 1/2 vanilla pod
- Generous 1/3 cup whole fresh milk
- 7 oz (200 g) white chocolate
- 7 oz (200 g) whipping cream
- Mint

For the jelly, boil the juice from the limes and the lemon with mineral water and sugar for a few minutes. Add a sheet of gelatin, presoftened and squeezed dry. Divide it between the glasses and add a few slices of grapefruit (all rind and pith removed) or raspberries, then leave them to set in the fridge.

For the mousse: Split and scrape the seeds from the vanilla pod and leave it to infuse in the cold milk for a few hours, then strain. Soften the remaining gelatin in cold water. Bring the milk almost to a boil and dissolve the squeezed-out gelatin sheet in it. Melt the chocolate in a bain-marie, then add the milk in three batches, emulsifying it briskly with a spatula to give a smooth glossy texture. The mixture should be warm, so reheat it if necessary. When it has reached between 95 and 105 °F (35 and 40°C), fold in the whipped cream in two batches, then the finely grated rind of a lime. Leave it to cool, and squeeze it onto the top of the jelly using a piping bag. Chill in the fridge. When you are ready to serve it, fill the glasses with slices of grapefruit or raspberries and mint.

cooks: Grandma Huguette, who quickly throws together a meal for fifteen out of virtually nothing, but worthy of a wedding feast. Grandma Lina with her gourmet dishes, and Mom with her great ideas and menus that delighted us as children. Not forgetting Daddy, the former pastry chef who's nobody's fool!

Advice from the blogger
Enjoy yourselves! Be passionate and you will inspire passion!

A few examples of dishes
Thrush kebabs, country salad, scrambled eggs with truffle, anchovy and garlic dip, zucchini mille-feuille, panfried milk cap mushrooms, breaded porcini mushrooms, lots of different soups, pheasant terrine with pistachios, tagine, stuffed cabbage with haddock puree, bouillabaisse, garlic mayonnaise, jams, Guy Savoy's strawberry tart, cocktail pastries, macaroons with candied chestnut cream…

What does that mean in an average day?
It means buying in loads every day, believe me, and this takes an incredible amount of time for someone as disorganized as I am! They laugh at me and my obsession with taking a photo of all my dishes. But it's my great passion, so I'm not giving it up!

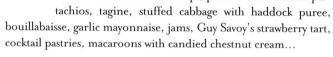

What's on the menu today?
A sundry mix just like me, in which Provence and Italy are both represented, thanks to Loulou and my parents.

My little weakness
Almonds in every shape and form, including face cream!

A white witch's cauldron
Poached pears
with nutty Saint-Agur cream

When I was devoid of inspiration, my mother came up with this idea for me. It is a simple yet effective recipe. We tested it on the family, and even my dad (who's not a great fan of sweet and sour things) loved it. I think the spices infused in the wine really give that added extra to this dish. Thank you, Mom.

Serves 4
· I clove
· Nutmeg
· 2 cups red wine
· 2 large Bartlett pears
· 2 oz (60 g) Saint Agur blue veined cheese
· 20 walnuts
· I cup whipping cream
· Salt and pepper

Start by adding a pinch of pepper, the clove and a little grated nutmeg to the wine, then heat it slowly. Peel the pears and cut them in half. Bring the wine to a boil and add the pears. Cook gently, turning the pears over carefully now and again, for about 15–20 minutes until the wine becomes syrupy and the pears are cooked (test by inserting the point of a knife, which should go in easily). Hollow out the center of the pears and keep the flesh you have removed. Chill the pears. Meantime crumble the cheese and roughly crush three quarters of the walnuts. Next prepare the whipped cream by carefully adding the crumbled cheese, crushed walnuts, and the pear flesh chopped into little cubes. Add salt and pepper. Stuff the pears with the mixture and garnish with the remaining walnuts.

Rabbit in cider with stuffed prunes and caramelized onions with wild savory

I had already made rabbit in beer, so why not with cider? And while we are at it, why not stuff the prunes with the breast instead of the other way round? And why not bring out the sweet and sour side of this recipe by serving it with caramelized onions? A hint of Provence with the wild savory, and that does the trick!

Serves 4
- 1 rabbit
- Flour
- Generous ? stick butter
- 9 oz (250 g) large prunes, pits removed
- 4 oz (100 g) smoked bacon pieces
- Wild savory
- 2 carrots
- 12 onions
- 4 cups dry cider
- 1 bouquet garni
- Olive oil
- 1 tbsp honey
- Salt and pepper

Cut the rabbit into portions and coat them with flour. Melt the butter in a casserole dish, and brown the rabbit breast pieces. Stuff each prune with a little of the breast meat. Brown the rest of the rabbit and the bacon pieces. Add half of the savory. When the meat is golden brown, add the carrots and 3 finely chopped onions, and brown them as well. Then add the cider and bouquet garni and season with salt and pepper. Leave to simmer for about 30 minutes. Prepare the caramelized onions and savory by finely slicing the remaining onions. Brown them in a little olive oil and honey, then season. Add the rest of the savory and cook until the onions become sticky and caramelized. After the rabbit has cooked for 30 minutes, add the stuffed prunes and cook for a further 15–30 minutes, depending on the size of the rabbit. Arrange the serving plates with a portion of rabbit basted with the cooking juice, a few prunes, and the caramelized onions.

Melon confit panna cotta on a Provencal candy mousse

This dessert is clearly inspired by my background: Provence and Italy. Panna cotta is an Italian dessert I am particularly fond of. As for melon and Provencal candy, you can't avoid them in Aix! You can replace the melon with any other fruit confit, of course. It's not an easy recipe, but it's worth the effort.

Panna cotta (for 4)

· I sheet gelatin
· Generous I cup whipping cream
· Scant I/2 cup superfine sugar
· 2 slices of melon confit

For the mousse

· I I/2 sheets gelatin
· 4 Provencal candies ("calisson"— almond and candied fruit in a paste, covered with icing)
· Generous I/3 cup milk
· I egg yolk
· 2 tbsp superfine sugar
· I/8 cup flour
· Generous I/3 cup whipping cream
· I tbsp icing sugar

The day before, soften the gelatin in a bowl of cold water. Bring the cream and sugar to a boil. Add the softened gelatin and whisk it well. Add the finely diced melon confit. Pour the mixture into 4 ramekin dishes. Chill for about 6 hours. When the panna cotta is well set, prepare the candy mousse. Soften the gelatin in a bowl of cold water. Finely chop the Provencal candy and bring the milk to a boil. In the meantime beat the egg yolk and sugar until pale and creamy. Mix in the flour. Pour in the milk, whisk, and heat very gently. Remove from the heat as soon as it starts to boil. Mix in the squeezed-out gelatin and then the candy. Leave it to cool down. Whip the cream and add the confectioner's sugar at the end. Carefully fold the cream into the (completely) cooled custard. Then pour it onto the panna cotta. Allow it to set in the fridge for at least 4 hours. Carefully remove it from the bowl or serve this dessert in individual glasses.

Apples in Calvados served in a sundae glass

Quick and effective. That's how I would sum up this recipe, which I made one Sunday when the urge for something sweet came over me, without any desire to spend hours in the kitchen. Of course you can liven it up a little with lots of different things like a crushed cookie base or chocolate shavings on top. Let your imagination run riot...

Serves 4
- 3 tbsp Calvados
- 2 tbsp soft brown sugar
- 2 tbsp orange juice
- 2 large apples
- Generous 1 cup whipping cream
- Whole hazelnuts and almonds for decoration

Mix the Calvados, brown sugar, and orange juice in a bowl. Cut the apples into pieces and leave them to marinate in the mixture for about an hour. Then put the apples and the juice into a pan and cook gently until the apples are caramelized. Whip up the cream. Leave the apples to cool. Line the bottom of the glasses with some apple and juice, then at the last moment put the cream on top and decorate with whole hazelnuts or almonds.

 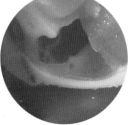

Emmanuèle's banana skins

My adventures and misadventures
in the kitchen, of a gourmet and gluttonous nature

Emmanuèle
(Lille),

a bookseller with
an appetite for life
and plenty of cravings

Why this blog?

A native of Bordeaux through and through (a disorganized one?), I had had enough of chasing after my endless notebooks and Post-Its whenever I had the urge to pen a new recipe. Especially when these pieces of paper had the bizarre knack of disappearing just when I needed them! I also wanted to record my blunders, including photographic evidence (table decorations, disasters, and a few recipes from nowhere).

**My little
weakness**
Sweet and sour,
crunchy and
smooth—contrasts!

What kind of cuisine is it?

My banana skins is hopefully about a playful kind of cooking that is also creative, funny, colorful, unstructured, often sweet and sour, sometimes risky, unconventional, not very traditional (down with "Grandma's home cooking"), easy to do, and based on ingredients that are easy to find.

A few examples of dishes

Summertime canapes; quavering apple and pear turnovers with meringue clouds; scallop kebabs wrapped in bacon on a bed of two tone veggie tagliatelli; flaky pastries singalong Southern style; zucchini charlotte with beef; fruity tagine with lamb, prunes, and apricots; multicolored beef; shallot and pistachio tart; cheeseburger deluxe; tuna-pepper croquettes; stewed peaches with violet whipped cream and spicy cookie topping; shooby-doo-wah tart; creamy strawberry crunch; melting but collapsing citrus cake; chocolate bouquets; strawberry candy mousse…

What does that mean in an average day?

I have reached the stage of being organized (almost) but am incapable of following a recipe to the letter! That results in a whirling carousel style of cooking, clutching utensils and clutching at the recipe!

What's on the menu today?

This menu takes us on a journey through sparkling, creamy undergrowth, only to plunge into a subtle, tender fish parcel accompanied by a velvety sauce. By way of dessert, we encounter a ray of melting crunchy brilliance, and finally we curl up in a whirlwind of chocolate and pastry.

Advice from the blogger

Reinvention, surprises, fun, and sharing. Anything that makes me jump for joy, drool at the mouth, or gives me pleasure deserves a spot on my blog!

Creamy soup
from the merry undergrowth

Have you just survived a downpour? Then go for this wonderfully comforting soup. An ultrasmooth mushroomy soup, thanks to that lovely, creamy cheese, The Laughing Cow (you might have guessed!) bringing a milky touch to a smooth appetizer.

Serves 4

- 1 garlic clove
- 1 shallot
- 1 red onion
- 1/8 stick butter
- 4 oz (125 g) white button mushrooms
- 4 oz (125 g) chanterelle mushrooms
- 1 2/3 cups water
- 1/2 chicken stock cube
- 2 portions of cheese spread (such as The Laughing Cow)
- Salt and pepper
- A few croutons for garnish (optional)

Brown the garlic, shallot, and onion, all finely chopped, in the butter for 5 minutes. Clean, slice, and season the mushrooms, then add them to the onion mix. Continue to cook for a good 5 minutes. Add the water and half a chicken stock cube, cover and cook for 15 minutes. Add the Laughing Cow cheese. Blend well and adjust the seasoning. Serve with a few croutons.

Emmanuèle's banana skins
Vanilla turbot parcels with black rice and red lentils

A dish to wow your guests. If you are entertaining your boss, the bank manager, a world leader, or your "significant other," then what are you waiting for—this elegant parcel is just what you are looking for. You'll dazzle them all!

Serves 4
- 1/2 stick softened butter
- 4 vanilla pods
- 4 turbot fillets
- 1 1/3 cup whipping cream
- Lemon juice
- 1 cup black rice
- 1 cup red lentils
- A few threads of saffron
- Salt and pepper

Work the butter into a paste and add the black seeds from the vanilla pods (open these and scrape the seeds out). Keep the pods to one side. Place the fish fillets on sheets of wax paper and spread the vanilla butter over them. Add salt and pepper. Close up the parcels and bake them in the oven for about 20 minutes at 350 °F (180 °C). Pour the cream and a little lemon juice into a small pan and let the vanilla pods infuse in it for 15 minutes. Season. Cook the rice and the lentils separately. When the parcels are ready, place them on hot plates, pour over the vanilla cream, and garnish with a few threads of saffron. Serve with the rice and lentils.

Look and taste

*One blog for indiscriminate foodies
and another for allergy sufferers*

Anne
(Bordeaux),
a creative chef who's into
food and eats everything

Why this blog?

After completing business studies I worked for about ten years before devoting myself to my family. Day by day I made good use of my time, allowing me to concentrate on my real passion—cooking. I started by setting up a simple web site so that I could keep track of my recipes.

It was only later that the idea of a blog took shape. This was partly because it was easy to set up, but more importantly I was then able to forge strong links with surfers who love to cook. Thus Look and Taste was born. As a mother of a child with allergies, a few months later I created the Look and Taste site for allergy sufferers as a way of helping desperate parents find recipes for their children. The point is to show that leaving things out of food does not mean it has to be boring.

My little weakness
Homemade bread, a tradition in my family pursued with passion.

Dedication
To Daddy Bear, without whom none of this would be possible, to Miss Bear who is interested in and passionate about everything, and to Baby Bear who makes a huge contribution to my creativity.

What kind of cuisine is it?

Simple and hearty southern cooking, more savory than sweet. In Blog 1, my specialty is bread in all shapes and forms. In Blog 2 are recipes that are free from gluten, eggs, and milk.

A few examples of dishes

Sea bass parcels with peppers, zucchini in batter with mint and mozzarella, flatbread with bacon pieces, Swedish cinnamon rolls, veal ribs Normandy style, oven baked lamb shoulder, black risotto with shrimp and fennel… not forgetting about 60 recipes for different types of bread.

What does that mean in an average day?

A permanent state of curiosity about what I'm eating and buying, children who aren't always overjoyed at trying new stuff, a delighted and patient husband, a budget with cookbooks at the top, and meeting lots of nice people—you, the reader (a moving experience), bloggers (it's as if you've always known them, we share so much in common), other aficionados of cooking, and so on.

What's on the menu today?

I'm taking you down to southwest France, an area where we live well and have first rate produce: duck, of course, but also lamb and vegetables from the region. To finish off, a Scottish dessert (the Aquitaine region was under British rule for a very long time) suitable for those allergic to eggs.

Advice from the blogger
Experiment and enjoy sharing.

Skewered duck breast with apples and cider

At home we love duck in all its forms. Of course, when you live in southwest France, it's as fresh as it gets! These little skewered duck breasts can be served as finger food for a hors d'oeuvre or a buffet, but they can also act as a main dish on a bed of mixed green salad, for example. This recipe is very quick and simple to make. You can substitute another chile for the Basque chile pepper if you do not have this, or you can use cumin for equally good results.

Serves 4

- 2 cooking apples
- 11 oz (300 g) duck breast slices
- 1 knob of butter
- Generous 1 cup cider
- Sea salt
- Basque chile pepper (optional)

Peel the apples and make little scoops using a melon baller. Cut the duck slices down the middle lengthwise. Wrap each apple ball in a slice of duck, holding it together with a cocktail stick. Melt the butter in a nonstick frying pan and, when hot, seal the duck and apple skewers. Cook on high heat for 2–3 minutes, then turn over and continue cooking for another minute. Then add 2–3 tablespoons of cider to make a sauce with the cooking juices and arrange on the serving dish right away. Add the sea salt and sprinkle with chile pepper. Serve immediately.

Pumpkin cappuccinos

A cream soup that everyone in our house loves, a consensus rare enough to be worth mentioning. And what is more, it can be made very quickly. If you like, you can even chop the pumpkin into cubes in advance and put them in the freezer. On the day you want to use them, all you have to do is take out the pumpkin pieces and you're ready to make this recipe. When serving I leave everyone to grate some fresh nutmeg to taste onto their own plate.

Peel the pumpkin, clean it, and cut it into chunks of about 1 in (3 cm). Put the pumpkin pieces into a deep casserole dish along with the chicken stock cube and cover with milk almost to the top. Cook uncovered for about 20 minutes until the pumpkin has softened. Blend well with a food mixer. Fill the serving glasses up to about 1 in (3 cm) from the top. Add a thin layer of cream and lemon juice, and then grate some nutmeg over it. Serve immediately.

Serves 4
· 1 pumpkin, about 2 lb (1 kg) in weight
· 1 chicken stock cube
· 1 2/3 cups half cream milk
· Whipping cream mixed with a little lemon juice
· Nutmeg

Lamb shoulder with tarragon, fava beans, and potato fritters

We are very fortunate to have delicious lamb in our region. Recently I discovered fava beans, and I think their flavor goes well with lamb and tarragon. As for the potato fritters, well if you have children you will know as I do that things are always better when potatoes are included in the menu...

Serves 4

- 1 shoulder of lamb, about 1 3/4 lb (800 g) in weight
- 6 cloves garlic
- 1 tsp tarragon
- 2 tbsps olive oil
- 2 onions
- 1 carrot
- 3 cups fava beans (fresh or frozen if out of season)
- 6 potatoes
- Generous 1/2 stick butter
- Salt and pepper

Preheat the oven to 450 °F (230 °C). Prepare the lamb shoulder. Put it in a roasting dish, slip 2 garlic cloves into the joint and add 3 more cloves to the dish. Sprinkle with half a teaspoon of tarragon and season with salt and pepper. Drizzle with olive oil and 1/3 cup water. Roast in the oven for 35 to 40 minutes. Check when it is ready, which will depend on the weight of the shoulder joint and your own preference for the meat (medium rare, medium, well done...). Bring water to a boil in a large pot with some salt, and then add 1 onion, the carrot, the rest of the tarragon, and the fava beans. Cook for 7–8 minutes once it has come back to a boil. Peel the potatoes and roughly grate them. Grate an onion and the remaining garlic clove.

Mix well together and add some salt and pepper. Heat a little butter in a skillet, and add a quarter of the mixture, patting it down. Cook gently for 7–8 minutes, then turn it over to cook for a few more minutes on the other side. Repeat the process for the three remaining fritters. Carve the meat, arrange it on the plates, and serve immediately.

Spicy shortbread
with apple and tangerine compote

Shortbread is an ideal cake if you are allergic to eggs. No need to rack your brain for a substitute ingredient as it is not in the recipe to start with. I like to add spices to it as I feel they give it a bit of added zing! And as shortbread isn't exactly the lightest of cakes, I serve it with fruit compote.

For the shortbread

- 8 tbsp brown sugar
- 2 1/2 cups flour
- 1 tsp ground cinnamon
- 1/2 tsp ground ginger
- 2 sticks butter
  (replace with margarine
  if you are allergic to milk)
- Confectioners' sugar for
  decoration

For the compote

- 8 Granny Smith apples
- 1/8 stick butter
- 6 tangerines
- 1 tsp ground cinnamon

Preheat the oven to 320 °F (160 °C). Mix the sugar, flour, and spices. Add the butter, cut into small cubes. Rub the mixture between your fingers to make a crumb texture, then pull it together into a smooth dough. If necessary moisten your hands with a little water. Roll out the dough into a circle about 8 in (20 cm) in diameter and less than 1 in (about 1 cm) thick. Place it on a baking sheet and pinch it all over with your fingers to make little notches. Then gently cut the circle into 16 portions. You can also cut shapes out with a pastry cutter and then put them on the baking sheet covered in wax paper. Bake in the oven for 20–25 minutes until the edges are pale golden. To make the compote, peel and dice the apples, then brown them in butter with the juice of 3 tangerines and the cinnamon. Cook for 15 minutes, then add the tangerine segments to the warm compote.

SAVEURS SUCRÉES SALÉES

Sweet and sour sensations
All my kitchen stories and other stuff...

Véronique
(Évry),
a serious cheese addict
from the Pyrénées

Why this blog?
Discovering culinary blogs was like a revelation to me. I identified with these kitchen "foodies" who were publishing their recipes, culinary explorations, and favorite things, day in day out. Mad about cooking since the age of 8 and having amassed nearly 30 years' worth of recipes in notebooks, files, and other backup methods, I said to myself "I could do that too," and that's how sweet and sour sensations came about. To begin with, I thought the blog would at least be of interest to my friends, who could then retrieve my recipes more easily. Then the circle gradually widened and perfect strangers came into my virtual kitchen and my life. Some of these have turned into real friends from all over the world—one of the incredible thing about blogs!

> **Advice from the blogger**
> Get used to eating things cold! Photo sessions and hot dishes are not exactly compatible, but it's all worth the effort.

What kind of cuisine is it?

In my virtual kitchen you'll find reworkings of the classics, a lot of sweet and sour dishes, variations on a lot of recipes (usually meaning that sweet becomes sour, and vice-versa)… and you will also find out about the flavors of the mountain region I come from, the Pyrénées.

A few examples of dishes

Fig quiche; mussels in cashew crumble; spicy layer bread with gorgonzola and figs; tuna charlotte and panna cotta with bell peppers; strawberries in geranium aspic with fennel preserve, little cushions of Camembert, and wallflowers; pumpkin and pistachio crumble; cake on a spit; white chocolate ice cream; cocoa nibs with Basque chile pepper; almond milk jelly with thyme and rose shortbread...

What does that mean in an average day?

The best, or sometimes the worst, for my family who are faced with unnamed (and unidentifiable) dishes on their plates. I would like to thank Alain (my husband), Nicolas and Pierre (my children) for their patience and (mostly) constructive feedback, and my parents Joseph and Annie, who taught me about the flavor and value of good produce.

What's on the menu today?

My little weakness
Cheese, cheese, and more cheese! Especially unpasteurised farm cheese, and always as an accompaniment to sweet and sour desserts. When I taste a cheese for the first time, I immediately think of what it would go well with, the next time it finds its way to my plate!

This menu is very typical of my kind of cooking and the ingredients I love. You'll find combinations that are rarely found together (and sometimes surprising), then of course a cheese done "my way," but also a little chocolate dessert that I hope will be one of your own classic recipes one day!

Lemon-scented rabbit rillettes

This recipe pays homage to my father, the Paté Professor! Well, Dad, does this student come even close to the standards of perfection of the master? Be that as it may, the creamy texture of this pate will melt your heart and the scent will carry you off to far and distant lands...

Serves 4

- 1/2 rabbit (1 portion each of saddle, front, and back legs)
- 2 cups water
- 1 large sprig of fresh green peppercorns
- 1/2 tsp cumin
- 6 black peppercorns
- 1 tbsp freshly chopped lemongrass
- 4 kafir lime leaves (also known as cumbava, available in Asian grocers)
- 5 oz (130 g) goose fat
- Salt

A day in advance, put the rabbit pieces in a casserole dish with the water and all the spices. Bring to a boil, then cover, and leave it to cook slowly (simmering gently) for 1 1/2 hours. Then add the goose fat and continue to cook, still covered, for a further 1 1/2 hours. Remove from the heat and leave it to cool down. Take the meat from the bones and put it to one side. Strain the cooking stock, then return it to the casserole dish. Flake the rabbit meat with your fingers and add it to the casserole, then boil it for 15 minutes. Pour the mixture into individual ramekin dishes and leave them to cool to room temperature. Cover with plastic wrap and keep them in the fridge for 24 hours. Serve with lovely toasted country bread.

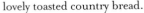

Haddock with kumquat vinaigrette and quinoa risotto

My mother is forever saying to me, "You need to eat more citrus fruit!" For once, I listened to her, and so just about every citrus fruit is included in this recipe. The result is an explosion of sunny flavors.

Serves 4
· 4 large haddock fillets

For the sauce
· 6 kumquats
· 1/2 red onion
· 1 tbsp fresh lemongrass
· 4 tbsps olive oil
· 2 tbsps soy sauce
· 1 tbsp lime juice
· 2 tbsp orange juice
· 1 heaped tsp brown sugar
· 1/2 tsp five-spice powder

For the risotto
· 1 small tsp lime peel
· 7 oz (200 g) quinoa
· 3 cups fish stock
· 1 small tsp dried lemon (available in Asian grocers)
· 4 tbsp whipping cream
· Salt and pepper

Prepare the sauce in advance: finely chop the kumquats, red onion, and lemongrass and mix these with all the other sauce ingredients. Leave it to marinate for 3 hours at room temperature. To make the risotto, chop the lime peel and blanch it in boiling water. Rinse the quinoa in cold water, then put it in a large saucepan with the fish stock, lemon, and blanched lime peel. Bring to a boil and cook for about 12 minutes. Strain a little off if there is too much fish stock left, then add the cream. Steam the haddock fillets, then keep them hot. Adjust the seasoning of the risotto if required, mix well, and put it into custard ring molds. Arrange a haddock fillet and a mound of risotto on each plate and coat with the citrus vinaigrette.

Tartlets with Munster cheese and blackcurrant

Serves 4

- I cup brown sugar, loosely packed
- 4 tbsp orange juice
- 2 cups fresh or frozen blackcurrants
- I tsp licorice powder
- I roll of puff pastry
- I Munster cheese from the farm
- Oil

Cheese or dessert? Why not both! This classical dilemma is resolved thanks to this happy marriage. Elegant puff pastry covered with blackcurrant compote, topped with oozing Munster cheese. And that's just to start!

Preheat the oven to 400 °F (200 °C).

Prepare the blackcurrant compote. Put the sugar, orange juice, and blackcurrants into a pan and bring to a boil. Lower the heat and cook uncovered for about 20 minutes, stirring regularly. When it has finished cooking, add the licorice powder. Mix well and leave it to cool down to room temperature. Roll out the puff pastry and cut out 4 circles or squares. Put them on a baking tray covered with lightly oiled wax paper. Then put another sheet of wax paper on top of the pastry, followed by another baking sheet, to prevent the puff pastry from rising. Bake in the oven for about 15 minutes, keeping an eye on it as it cooks. When the pastry is golden, take it out of the oven. Spread the blackcurrant compote over the bottom of each pastry, then lay slices of cheese on top. Put it back into the oven at high heat for a few minutes to melt the cheese slightly. Serve hot.

Iced chocolate
with tarragon and homemade nougat

We are all familiar with chocolate and mint, or chocolate and basil, but chocolate and tarragon? This aromatic herb with a big personality goes beautifully with milk chocolate. So I turned them into an iced version, as a subtly sweet appetizer with a velvety aniseed taste. A taste to die for!

For 4 glasses of chocolate
· 2/3 cup milk
· 4 tbsp whipping cream
· I tbsp dried tarragon
· 3 oz (70 g) grated milk chocolate

For the nougat
· I tsp dried tarragon
· I/2 cup superfine sugar
· 2 tbsp chopped almonds
· Oil

To make the nougat candy: blend the dried tarragon into a powder using a food mixer, then put to one side. Put the sugar in a non-stick pan and dry fry it until caramelized. When golden in color, add the almonds and the ground tarragon. Continue cooking for a few seconds, enough time for the caramel to coat the almonds and become a shade darker. Pour onto a greased marble slab or a waxed cloth. Lay a sheet of oiled wax paper on top and, using a rolling pin, press down the nougat until it is a thin sheet. Remove the oiled paper and leave it to cool. Pour the milk, cream, and tarragon into a pan. Bring to a boil, then leave it to infuse for about 10 minutes. Strain the milk, crushing the tarragon to release its full flavor. Return the milk to the pan, add the grated chocolate, and bring slowly to a boil. Cook for a further 5 minutes until the mixture has thickened, stirring continuously. Whip it up into a mousse using a whisk, then pour it into individual glasses. Leave it to reach room temperature, then put it in the fridge. Break up the nougat. Serve the iced chocolate with a piece of nougat.

Station gourmande

Découvrir les saveurs et mets du monde

Gourmet Grand Central

A different take on cooking

Anne (Paris),
gastronomic
globetrotter

Why this blog?

After working for 18 years in a large audit office, I wanted to turn my great passion—cooking—into my career and find out what goes on behind the scenes in the world of gastronomy. You need an apprenticeship for this, however, so I went to the Ferrandi cooking school. Now I would like to put my plans into practice and open a nice friendly restaurant in Paris. I love to share and pass on what I know, so I thought a blog would be a fantastic means of communication. In return I have received lots of feedback from readers which I have found touching, moving, and inspiring; and I love going into my kitchen to concoct new recipes.

My little weakness
Sweet and sour—I love to combine ingredients, mixing together flavors to create recipes and share them with you.

What kind of cuisine is it?

Different products are the main focus in my cooking—dressing them in flavors from faraway places, contrasting and fusing them with each other to achieve what I hope is an unforgettable and rich combination. The Mediterranean region is the original base for me, but I have also expanded my horizons as far as Asia. I am constantly substituting less well known or used ingredients for the more common ones. I salt some of my dishes with nuoc-mâm (a Southeast Asian fish sauce), I have at least five types of oil in my cupboards (two of which are olive oils), and I play around with herbs and spices (galanga, lemongrass, licorice…).

A few examples of dishes

Kiwi served in a glass, chicken and cashew nuts; maki paella; cream cheese with fennel and licorice; monkfish cheek curry; skate wings with Camembert; foie gras candy; bell pepper and saffron jam; nougat mousse; apple and cinnamon cake; spaghetti with chopped tomatoes and pomegranate; mango and zucchini salad; orange and almond cake; sea bream tartare with cherries; guinea fowl tagine with damson plums...

> **Advice from the blogger**
>
> Get cooking, make a mess of it, start again, share and learn, introduce people to new things, and make their mouths water... With fresh ingredients and just a little time, home cooking can be done.

What does that mean in an average day?

Always having a notebook and a pen in my bag, a notebook at home with lists, sketches, stains, and things crossed out... , a camera in my hand and understanding friends! Quite often I go out to get groceries without the slightest idea of what I am going to make, then I let my imagination wander across the shelves. That was how I came upon the idea of a hot and cold dish with cottage cheese one day, for instance.

What's on the menu today?

I wanted to use it to introduce you to my culinary world, where straightforward techniques blend with tastes imported from other countries. The flavor of the ingredients will not be tampered with, but it will stimulate your appetite for a gastronomic journey at mealtimes. The different techniques are explained on the blog in the section "The Knack."

Fresh crab spring rolls
with hot orange vinaigrette

An old dream became reality, thanks to writing the book. Love at first taste.

Serves 4

- 1 carrot
- 1 zucchini
- 1 orange
- 1 leek
- 1/4 lb (100 g) beansprouts
- 1 tsp palm sugar
- 1/2 tbsp nuoc-mâm (fish sauce)
- 2 tbsps rice vinegar
- 8 sheets of filo pastry
- 1/2 cup melted butter
- 7 oz (200 g) flaked crab
- Fresh coriander
- 1 bunch Chinese chives
- 2 tbsps olive oil
- salt

With a vegetable peeler, slice the peeled carrot, zucchini, and orange. Cut them into julienne strips along with a few leek leaves, so that you have fine sticks the same size as the beansprouts. Separately, boil the carrot and beansprouts in salted water (20 seconds) and the zucchini and leek (10 seconds). Blanch the orange strips three times, changing the water after each boiling. Dissolve the sugar in the fish sauce and vinegar in a bowl. Preheat the oven to 375 °F (180 °C). Lay two sheets of filo on top of each other and brush them with melted butter. Put the juliennes, beansprouts, and crab on the pastry sheets, leaving less than a half inch (1 cm) at the bottom and about twice as much at the side edges. Roll up halfway, fold in the edges, then finish rolling up, brushing with butter as you go. Make up the three other spring rolls. Bake in the oven for 15 minutes, turning over halfway through cooking. Squeeze the orange, reducing the juice by two thirds in a pan. Finely chop the coriander and chives. Add them to the sauce in the bowl with the reduced orange juice and olive oil, and then pour the sauce over the hot spring rolls.

Fish in orange and ginger sauce with curried rice

An easy recipe accompanied by unusual, crunchy rice. My friends have nearly all made it part of their repertoire.

Serves 4

- 1 1/8 sticks butter
- 4 shallots
- 1 oz (30 g) piece of root ginger
- 1 unwaxed lemon
- 4 fish fillets
- 1 1/2 cups fish stock
- 1 1/2 cups rice
- 1 tbsp olive oil
- 1 tbsp mustard seeds
- 15 curry leaves (not powder)
- 1 orange
- Coarse salt

Preheat the oven to 450 °F (220 °C). Cut the butter into tiny cubes and put them in the freezer. Peel and chop the shallots. Peel and grate the ginger. Remove the peel from the lemons and cut them into julienne strips. Blanch them by plunging them into boiling water three times (do not add salt to the water and change it each time). Put a layer of shallots and ginger into the dish. Add the fish fillets and half cover with fish stock. Bake in the oven for 10 minutes. Cook the rice. Squeeze the lemon. Put a little olive oil in a frying pan and roast the mustard seeds and curry leaves, then remove the pan from the heat and add the lemon strips. Drain the rice and mix in the curry and lemon juice. Season to taste. When the fish is cooked, strain the cooking juices and reduce in a pan by two thirds. Squeeze the orange and add it to the pan, reducing it down once again. Remove the pan from the heat and add a quarter of the butter, beating the sauce with a whisk, then mix in the rest of the butter and continue to whisk until it has all melted. Arrange the fish fillets, sauce, and rice on the plates.

Mango mille-feuille with lychee mousse

A fresh and tasty little dish with accents of Asia. I am particularly fond of the combination of two fruits, shown to best advantage by a European recipe with the added magic of Asian hot and cold style.

Preheat the oven to 450 °F (220 °C). Cut three circles per person out of the puff pastry. Put the circles on a nonstick tray and wedge a second tray on top so that the pastry does not rise. Bake in the oven for 10 minutes. Cream the egg yolks and sugar in a copper bowl. Sift the flour and add it to the mixture. Heat the milk and mix it into the egg and sugar. Put it all in a pan to heat and then boil for 3 minutes. Pour into a wide dish and chill in the fridge. Peel the lychees, removing the pits, and then blend them (saving 4 for decoration). Strain the puree and pour the juice into the chilled cream mousse. Add 7/8 of the creamy butter to the cream. Peel and dice the mangoes. Brown them in the remaining butter and four-spice. Sprinkle the pastry circles with confectioners' sugar and caramelize them on each side under the grill. All you need to do now is put it together: puff pastry, mango, mousse (with a piping bag), and puff pastry. Sprinkle with confectioners' sugar and put one lychee on top of each for decoration.

Serves 4
- 2 sheets puff of pastry
- 3 egg yolks
- 3 tbsp superfine sugar
- 1/3 cup flour
- Generous 1 cup milk
- 9 oz (250 g) lychees (reserve 4 lychees to decorate)
- 1 stick butter, softened
- 2 mangoes
- A pinch of four-spice
- Confectioners' sugar

A glass of tea

A different way to end the meal, with something light, smooth, and aromatic. The ginger preserve makes it explode in your mouth. I made several attempts before finding the right amount for each ingredient.

Serves 4
· 1 oz (30 g) galanga
· 1 lemongrass stalk
· 30 jasmine pearls
· or 1 tsp jasmine tea
· 2 tsps brown sugar
· 1/2 tsp agar-agar
· 4 lychees
· Ginger preserve

Peel the galanga and cut into two pieces. Remove the outer leaf from the lemongrass, then split the stalk and crush it with the flat side of a knife. Heat the galanga and lemongrass in 1 1/2 cups water. When it starts to boil, add the jasmine or tea. Allow it to cool to bring out all the aromas. Strain it, bring to a boil, sweeten, and add the agar-agar. There are two ways of serving it: put the lychees at the bottom of the glass and pour in the tea, then allow it to set it the fridge; or pour some tea into the bottom of the glass, leave to set for 5–10 minutes, put in the lychees, and pour in the rest of the tea before putting it in the fridge. Before serving, sprinkle little pieces of diced ginger preserve on top.

" Tarzile.com

LA VIE EST... SIMPLE!

tarzile.com

Tarzile

Sylviane (Montreal, Quebec),
lover of figs and arugula

You can never have enough fruit, vegetables, or desserts!

Why this blog?

To share my passions with members of my family who live far away from me. I wanted to offer them recipes that were easy to do when you get in from work, when starving kids are nibbling anything they can find, shouting "What's for dinner? I'm hungry!" Thanks to the blog, my family has expanded and I am lucky to be rubbing shoulders with folk who are as mad and passionate about food as I am.

What kind of cuisine is it?

Tarzile.com takes its inspiration from everyday life, from women who have gone before me, and from the region I come from. A fusion of French, English, and American influences, this land is an endless source of inspiration. Tarzile.com is about simple cooking, and enjoys taking a fresh look at it in light of new trends. Adding dried figs soaked in rose water to the humble bread pudding. Uniting the old and the new. Taking advantage of cuisine from around the world to give me richer memories in the future. Tarzile.com prepares our traditional vegetables in a simple way. Of course, this doesn't stop us celebrating Christmas and Halloween in the old style.

My little weakness
Arugula in everything. In green soup, BLT sandwiches, party salads, and manicotti fillings. Arugula in a dessert? I'm thinking about it!

Advice from the blogger

Put up the recipes you like, even the simplest ones, and provide illustrations. Use natural light whenever possible. Halogen spots are a killer—they cut out all variations in shade. Bring out Grandma's crockery, especially the brightly colored pieces. Your photos will be brilliant and your dishes mouthwatering.

A few examples of dishes

Winter pesto of green vegetables with almonds; poutine (a Canadian speciality of french fries, curd cheese, and gravy) with foie gras cooked in a cloth; sugar tart; butter cookies with lavender; cream of zucchini soup with avocado.

What does that mean in an average day?

I am always on the alert, wondering what I might publish online. My camera is always near my kitchen unit. No one can start eating until I've taken the photo of the food. My flabbergasted neighbor seems to be getting increasingly concerned when he sees me photographing everything I put on the garden table. The thing I like most? Visitors to the site who try out a recipe and come back to express their appreciation. Very gratifying. Never mind the time I spend visiting the blogs of my cyberpals and finding out about their accomplishments, or the messages sent and received! I know I can always count on my cyberpals' knowledge. And that's invaluable.

What's on the menu today?

With this menu exuding the delicious smell of leaves in fall, you are cordially invited to celebrate the colors of the Quebec landscape in all its simplicity. Watch out for Esmeralda, our local witch!

Tarzile

Creamy soup made by the garden elves

"Not spinach," I can just hear the kids sighing. Yet it's an ideal elvish ingredient! What if we made a cream soup with it? Vegetables often go down better when presented in the form of a soup. The mixture of spinach and Swiss chard gives this creamy soup a vibrant color.

Serves 4
· 6 oz (170 g) fresh Swiss chard and spinach leaves
· 4 cups chicken stock
· 3/8 stick butter
· Scant 1/4 cup flour
· Ground Basque chile pepper
· Salt and pepper

Trim the chard, separating the leaves from the stalk: gently fold the leaf in two, keep holding it like this with one hand and, with the other, pull away the stalk. Keep the stalks to use for something else. Heat the stock and keep it hot. Melt the butter in a large pan. Add the flour, mixing well with a wooden spoon. Cook for a few minutes. Season with salt and pepper. Add the hot stock gradually, stirring continuously until the mixture is smooth. Continue to cook and stir for about 5 minutes until it thickens. Add the spinach and chard leaves. Cook uncovered for about 1 minute. or until the vegetables have wilted. Blend the soup in a mixer. Sprinkle with Basque chile pepper and serve immediately.

Osso bucco with fresh figs and cranberries

I love slowly stewed dishes, even better heated up! I have a real passion for fresh figs, and have tried introducing them to all sorts of sauces, including veal. To add a touch of spice to the fig and wine combination in this recipe, I have added cranberries, those tart little red berries so typical of our region and very popular during year-end festivities. If you cannot obtain cranberries, you can either leave them out or replace them with bilberries.

Serves 4
· Olive oil
· Butter
· 4 gray shallots
· 4 thick slices of knuckle of veal
· Flour
· Generous cup Muscat wine
· 6 fresh figs
· 1/2 cup fresh cranberries (optional)
· Salt and pepper

Preheat the oven to 350 °F (180 °C). Gently heat the olive oil and a knob of butter in a large ovenproof casserole. Brown the peeled and quartered shallots in the casserole. Coat the knuckle of veal pieces with flour and seal them immediately by cooking on each side for 2 minutes. Season the meat with salt and pepper. Add the wine. Cover and slip the casserole into the oven. Cook for 45 minutes. Take the casserole out of the oven, turn the meat over and add the quartered figs and the cranberries. Add some more wine if required. Put it back into the oven and cook for a further 45 minutes. The meat should fall off the bone when ready. Serve with pasta in butter or olive oil.

Esmeralda's white chocolate cake with pumpkin

Pumpkins—you can make soups and gratins with them, or even tarts and cakes. By adding white chocolate chips you get a fabulous cake fit for a party. A cake that Esmeralda the witch would be proud of.

Preheat the oven to 350 °F (180 °C). Cut the pumpkin in two and put the two halves on a baking tray covered with waxed paper. Lightly oil the flesh of the pumpkin. Bake in the oven until tender, or for 40–50 minutes. Leave it to cool, then scoop out the flesh with a spoon and blend it in a mixer. Add a little water if necessary to make the puree slightly runny. Measure out a generous cup of puree and keep the rest to use for something else. Grease a cake mold and dust with flour. Mix the eggs, oil, and vanilla in a bowl. Add the sugar and buttermilk, and mix until you have a smooth consistency. Add the pumpkin puree and mix well. In another bowl, mix the flour, baking powder, salt, cardamom, and bicarbonate. Add the chocolate chips. Amalgamate both mixtures. Pour into the mold and bake in the oven for about 40 minutes. Eat when it has cooled.

For a family size cake

- 1 pumpkin
- 1/2 cup sunflower or rapeseed oil
- 2 1/2 cups flour
- 2 eggs
- 1 tsp vanilla extract
- 3/8 cup sugar
- 1/2 cup buttermilk
- 1 tsp baking powder
- 1/2 tsp salt
- 1/2 tsp ground cardamom seeds
- 1/2 tsp bicarbonate of soda
- 3 oz (90 g) white chocolate chips

Mom's fudge candy with maple syrup

I am giving you the secret recipe for my mother's fudge candy. A delicious tidbit that is a MUST for the Christmas table. Guests will look pathetically disappointed if you don't provide this candy. It is important to use a sugar thermometer when making the fudge.

For 20 squares
- 1 2/3 cups maple syrup
- 1 cup brown sugar, loosely packed
- Generous cup whipping cream
- 1 pinch sea salt

In a high sided pan, pour in the maple syrup, sugar, cream, and sea salt. Stir continuously over low heat with a wooden spoon until the sugar has completely dissolved. If the sugar does not completely dissolve at this stage, you will get crystals in the candy. Once the sugar has dissolved, put the sugar thermometer in the pan. Increase to medium heat. Do not disturb the mixture until it has reached 244 °F (118 °C), or the "firm ball" stage. Then remove from the heat. Pour the mixture into a large metal bowl to make it cool down more quickly, with the thermometer still in it. Do not touch it. When the thermometer reads 113 °F (45 °C), stir with a wooden spoon until the mixture becomes dull. Then pour it into a mold lined with waxed paper. Sprinkle with a few grains of sea salt if you like. Put the mold in the fridge. When the candy is firm, cut into little squares. Serve with an espresso or green tea.

TASCA DA ELVIRA
CUISINE DU PORTUGAL & D'AILLEURS...

Elvira's diner
Feasting on fado

Elvira (Tomar, Portugal),
a fan of Fernando
Pessoa's poems

Why this blog?

As I love to cook, I was always cutting and pasting lots of recipes on my computer over the years. My husband suggested the idea of sharing them on my personal blog at that point. My recipes met with great success, so I decided to start a blog dedicated just to cooking. And besides, I wanted to tell everyone about the wonderful diversity of Portugese cuisine, still largely unrecognized beyond its borders. This is true of many countries, where there are communities of Portugese origin that are keen to find out about the culture of their homeland.

What kind of cuisine is it?

Elvira's diner is a blog that is basically dedicated to both traditional and modern Portugese cooking, and more besides. My blog purports to be representative of the way people cook in Portugal today, with all the influences of other Portugese-speaking countries and even international gastronomy as well. And as my husband and I have traveled quite widely, we are also keen to share our exotic discoveries and cooking experiences, inevitably influenced by France, the country in which we spent most of our lives. So Elvira's diner is a pretty cosmopolitan zone,

My little weakness
All the homemade produce from the little village I live in and the surrounding area, made just the way my grandparents use to: fresh sheeps' milk cheese, oli oil, raw smoked ham, lean chourico sausage, wine from small vineyards…

amenable to all sorts of cooking according to the seasons and what we feel like. From the ubiquitous salt cod to tasty morsels for eating with a baguette. Recipes that are always easy... but taste great!

Advice from the blogger

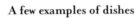

A culinary blog is really done for personal enjoyment. I am not trying to be fantastically original or to lay to the gallery, still less to think of myself as a great chef. Stay true to your own particular style of cooking and only make what really makes your own mouth water.

A few examples of dishes

Baked salt cod, Porto style; thinly sliced poultry with coffee sauce; Brazilian lemon tart; chicken curry with zucchini; lamb stew; Portugese stuffed crab; potato fritters with chourico sausage; cream custards...

What does that mean in an average day?

Since I've been doing Elvira's diner our food has become far more inventive and wide ranging. It's rare for us to eat the same dish twice in the same month! My shopping lists are much more organized because I think about my menus in advance, which really wasn't the case before the blog.

What's on the menu today?

An invitation to discover contemporary Portugese cooking, spanning tradition and modernity—an appetizer that is a bit trendy, quite a traditional festive dish from central Portugal and desserts that are simple and typical, all flavored with the spices characteristic of the region.

Elvira's diner
Two veg and curd cheese tartlets

Serving this appetizer will be a winner… thanks not only to the contrast in colors and flavors, but also to the sweetness of the vegetables and the curd cheese which are delicately counterposed to the strong, spicy note of the herbs involved.

Steam the green beans and carrots separately. Add salt during the cooking. Reduce the vegetables into two purees. Soak the gelatin sheets in cold water. Bring the cream to a boil and remove from the heat. Squeeze out the gelatin and blend it into the cream using a whisk until it has dissolved completely. Beat the curd cheese until creamy. Mix the savory with the green beans, the finely grated orange rind with the carrots, then the mustard and herbs to the beaten cheese. Divide the cream equally between the two mixtures. Mix well. Add salt and pepper to taste. Lightly oil four individual ramekin dishes. Layer with the green bean mix, then the curd cheese, and finally the carrot mix, allowing it to set in the fridge between each layer. When assembled, leave them in the fridge to set. Before removing the tartlets from the dishes, briefly run the bottom of the ramekin dish under hot water. Turn the tartlets out onto the plates (preferably onto a bed of salad leaves) and garnish.

Serves 4
- 14 oz (400 g) green beans
- 2 2/3 cups carrots
- 10 sheets of plain gelatin
- 2/3 cup whipping cream
- 11 oz (300 g) sheeps' curd cheese
- 1 sprig of savory, chopped
- Zest of 1 orange
- 1 heaped tsp strong mustard
- 2 tbsps flat leaf parsley, chives and mint, chopped and mixed
- Oil
- Salt and pepper

Duck fricassee with cinnamon

The cuisine of central Portugal is the inspiration for this recipe, or to be more precise, the area around the town of Coimbra, where they love rich dishes. The aroma of cinnamon—which is used as much with savory as with sweet foods in Portugal—is combined with lemon to give a really festive feel to this dish.

Cut the duck into portions and season them with salt and pepper. Squeeze the juice of 1 lemon over them and leave for 1 hour. Preheat the oven to 400 °F (200 °C). Put the duck portions in an ovenproof dish. Sprinkle little pieces of butter over the duck meat. Bake in the oven for about 1 hour 10 minutes. Take off a little of the cooking juices and put it in a pan with the olive oil. Lightly brown the chopped onion in it. Add the duck and cinnamon stick. Fry the duck for a few seconds, then pour in 1 1/2 cups of water and leave it to simmer for 20 minutes. Separately, beat the egg yolks with some of the cooking juices and the juice of a half lemon. Blend this into the sauce, removed from the heat, stirring continuously until you get a creamy sauce. Adjust the seasoning. Sprinkle the dish with chopped parsley just before serving. Garnish with slices of lemon and serve with rice.

Serves 4
- 1 duck, weighing about 3 ? lb (1.5 kg)
- 2 lemons
- 2 tbsps butter
- 1 tbsp olive oil
- 1 onion
- 1 stick cinnamon
- 3 egg yolks
- 1 small bunch of flatleaf parsley
- 2 lb (900 g) rice
- Salt and pepper

Pears in dill

Light and subtly aromatic, this pear recipe is simplicity itself and is ideal for rounding off a substantial meal. It combines two Portugeses spices that are indispensable for making desserts—dill seeds and cinnamon.

Serves 4
· 6 small red pears
· 1 cinnamon stick
  (plus 4 for decoration—optional)
· 1 tbsp dill seeds
· 1 1/3 cups brown sugar, tightly
  packed
· 1 pinch salt

Wash the pears throroughly. Cut them in half lengthwise but do not peel them. Carefully remove the hard part in the middle containing the pits. Put the pears in a stoneware casserole dish or a copper pan. Cover them with 7/8 cup water. Add the cinnamon stick, dill seeds, pinch of salt, and a little sugar. Bring the mixture to a boil and cook for 10 minutes. Transfer the pears to individual serving dishes and strain the cooking juices. Add the sugar to the cooking juices and bring to a boil again. Stirring continuously with a whisk, continue to boil the juice until it is a golden syrup. Pour the syrup over the pears and sprinkle with a few dill seeds. Leave it to cool before serving. If you like, you can also add cinnamon sticks as decoration.

Chocolate melting moments
from Abrantes

Abrantes is a pretty town in central Portugal, sitting on the banks of the Tage river, bordering two regions rich in culinary traditions: Ribatejo and Beira Baixa. These are typical of family cooking in Portugal, where folk have too much respect for food to contemplate throwing any of it out. Stale bread is resurrected as tiny chocolate puddings that are a perfect accompaniment to the post-prandial ritual of coffee.

For 20 balls

· 9 oz (250 g) bread (the soft inside part)
· Scant 1 cup cocoa powder
· 7/8 cup superfine sugar
· 1 thimblefull brandy or Cognac
· 1 1/2 cups dessicated coconut

Put the bread, broken up into tiny pieces, into a fairly large container. Add the cocoa, sugar, brandy, and 7/8 cup water. Work all the ingredients together with your hands until the mixture is thoroughly blended. Form little balls out of the mixture and roll them in the dessicated coconut. Serve the chocolates in little molds lined with wax paper.

How the book came about

Nearly every blogger harbors the dream of publishing her own cookbook and this book is the product of just such a dream! *Véronique Chapacou* put together some ideas about that dream, with the suggestion that it should be a collaborative effort, and set about contacting the rest of our group. *Claire Chapoutot* and *Gloria Herpin* met with her to realize the project, with help from *Anne Rolland* during the startup phase. They were joined by eleven other participants, all just as enthusiastic: *Sylviane Beauregard*, *Dominique Bergès*, *Emmanuèle Carroué*, *Mijo D'Araujo*, *Frédérique Despature*, *Stéphanie Durand*, *Anne Lataillade*, *Elvira Mendes André*, *Jacqueline Mercorelli*, *Brigitte Munoz*, and *Aude Toniello*.

The initial idea was to do a "hard copy" of the culinary blog contents: some "choice cuts" from the virtual kitchens which would be available to everyone, especially those who do not have internet access. But this book is just as much the story of the meeting between this team of bloggers and the series editor, Raphaële Vidaling, who immediately had faith in the project. Each of the 15 bloggers created eight recipes, four of which were picked to make up the menus in this book. Every one of these women contributed her personality, her specialties, and knowledge in order to bring you previously unpublished recipes that still remain faithful to their author. They were then tried out and modified where necessary before being reformulated in their final version… the one you now have in your hands!